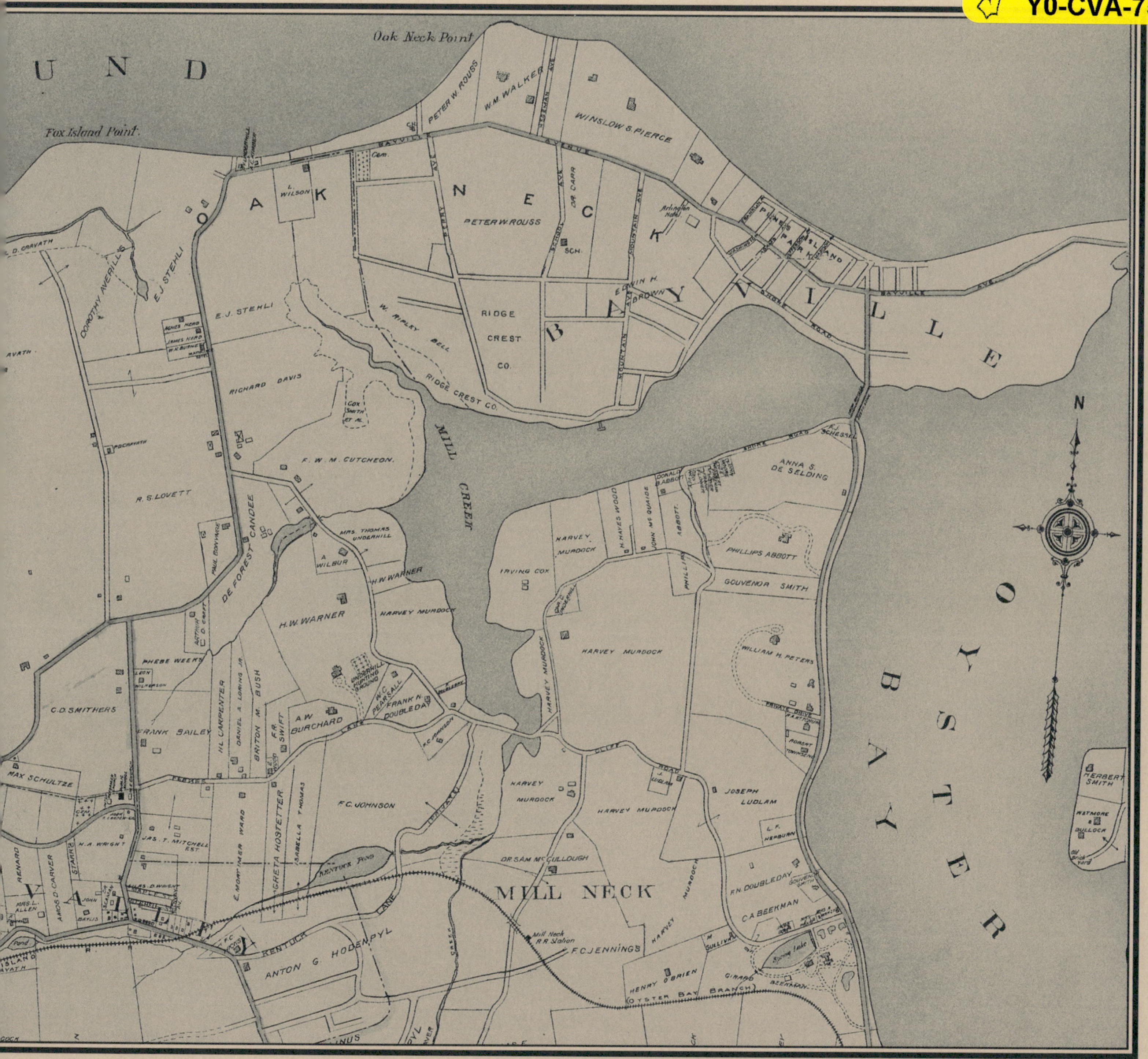

Oak Neck Point
UND
Fox Island Point
OAK NECK
BAYVILLE
PETER W. ROUSS
W. M. WALKER
WINSLOW S. PIERCE
L. WILSON
E. J. STEHLI
DOROTHY AVERILL
RIDGE CREST CO.
W. RIPLEY BELL
RICHARD DAVIS
F. W. M. CUTCHEON
R. S. LOVETT
DE FOREST CANDEE
MILL CREEK
ANNA S. DE SELDING
PHILLIPS ABBOTT
GOUVENOR SMITH
HARVEY MURDOCK
IRVING COX
H. W. WARNER
WILLIAM H. PETERS
OYSTER BAY
C. D. SMITHERS
FRANK BAILEY
A. W. BURCHARD
FRANK N. DOUBLEDAY
F. C. JOHNSON
MAX SCHULTZE
H. A. WRIGHT
JAS. T. MITCHELL EST.
E. MORTIMER WARD
GRETA HOSTETTER
ISABELLA T. HOMAS
Kentuck Pond
DR. SAM McCULLOUGH
MILL NECK
JOSEPH LUDLAM
F. N. DOUBLEDAY
C. A. BEEKMAN
ANTON G. HODENPYL
F. C. JENNINGS
HENRY O'BRIEN
Mill Neck R.R. Station
OYSTER BAY BRANCH
Spring Lake
HERBERT SMITH
N

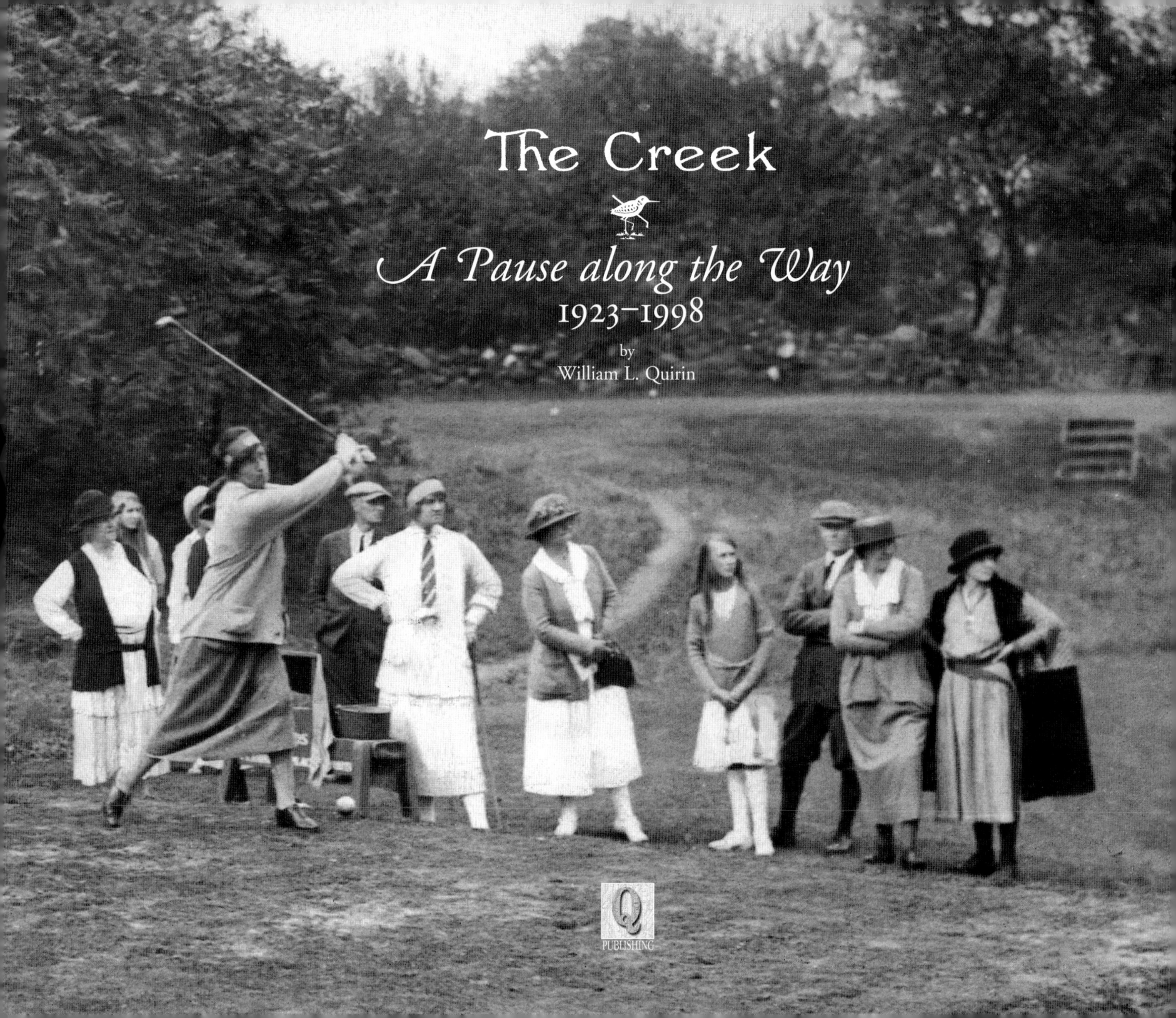

The Creek

A Pause along the Way
1923–1998

by
William L. Quirin

Main Clubhouse today

Copyright © 1998 by The Creek
All rights reserved, including the right to reproduce this work in any form whatsoever without permission in writing from the copyright holder, except for brief passages in connection with a review. For infomation, write:
Q Publishing, P.O. Box 561, Franklin, VA 23851
Debra Y. Quesnel, Owner and Publisher
Elizabeth B. Bobbitt, Creative Director

Library of Congress Cataloging-in-Publication Data
Quirin, William L.
 The Creek: a pause along the way, 1923-1998 / by William L. Quirin.
  p.   cm.
 ISBN 0-9665228-0-X
 1. Creek (Golf club: Locust Valley, N.Y.)--History. I. Title.
GV969.C74Q57 1998
796.352'06'8747245--dc21   98-33739
                                         CIP
Printed in Iceland

Table of Contents

	Foreword	7
Chapter 1	The American Mediterranean	9
Chapter 2	The Gold Coast	13
Chapter 3	Veraton	19
Chapter 4	A Quiet Club	23
Chapter 5	Titans	33
Chapter 6	A Macdonald Course	41
Chapter 7	The Beach	47
Chapter 8	Sailing Through Rough Waters	57
Chapter 9	Women's National	63
Chapter 10	The Cedar Creek Club	67
Chapter 11	The Racquets Renaissance	75
Chapter 12	The Indoor Facility	87
Chapter 13	"This Is a Golf Club"	95
Chapter 14	The Golf Course Restoration	107
	The Creek in Color	113
Chapter 15	The Gold Coast, Revisited	145
	Epilogue	150
	Appendices	151

The Dormie House today

Foreword

The history of The Creek links the Roaring Twenties to the Space Age. The past seventy-five years have seen dramatic changes: war and peace, social and economic upheaval, good times and bad. Though not unscathed, and certainly influenced by the tumultuous events of these years, The Creek has flourished and matured, has changed and come of age in its own way. Its "raison d'être" remains the same: outdoor sports, fine dining, and good fellowship.

This book is an attempt to capture, in print and in pictures, the fascinating people and events that have shaped the seventy-five-year life of our beloved club. To have it written as part of the celebration of our seventy-fifth anniversary, we are deeply indebted to two people. The first is member Donald J. Shea, who has devoted countless hours working closely with the author, researching the Creek's history and supervising the production. And, second, to author Bill Quirin, the historian for the Metropolitan Golf Association and author of several other club anniversary books, who has responded to Don's dedication with his own ardent commitment.

Finally, we are grateful to the many people who have shared their memories of The Creek in interviews and/or have contributed photographs and other memorabilia to enhance the book. They are formally acknowledged in the Appendix.

WILLIAM F. KENNY III

An 1860 painting showing the view from the top of Weir Hill (today's sixth tee)

CHAPTER I

The American Mediterranean

European civilization first reached Long Island by sea, the first explorers arriving by boat. Their pathway of discovery was Long Island Sound which, for many years, was called "The American Mediterranean."

Long Island Sound was "discovered" by Europeans in 1614 when the Dutchman, Adriaen Block, escaped through the treacherous currents of Hell Gate into previously uncharted waters. His vessel, *The Restless,* was the first American-built ship. His explorations took him along the Connecticut coast, indeed up the Connecticut River as far as what is now Hartford.

The first Dutch and English inroads along the Sound came after the Pequot War (1637), in which Captain John Underhill, among others, thoroughly defeated the warlike Indian tribe in Connecticut, thereby opening the shores of the Sound to settlement. The first major colony in Connecticut was at New Haven in 1638.

Eventually, the Connecticut settlers sailed across the Sound and explored Long Island's North Shore, establishing the first colony on Long Island at Southhold on the North Fork. Captain Underhill was among the early explorers.

The early settlers quickly came to appreciate the advantages of living in close proximity to the Sound. The sea provided an abundant supply of food, while the waters proved to be a quick mode of transportation, especially so at a time when overland travel was quite tedious.

In 1650 a dividing line between Dutch and English territory on Long Island was established in the vicinity of Oyster Bay. The English took complete control in 1664, and established duties on all goods shipped into Long Island. This led to a period of smuggling, and eventually piracy. Captain Kidd was appointed by the British government to stop the smuggling, and took advantage of his authority to become the most feared pirate of all, amassing a tremendous fortune before being caught and hanged.

The north shore of what is now Nassau County was once the home of the Matinecock, an

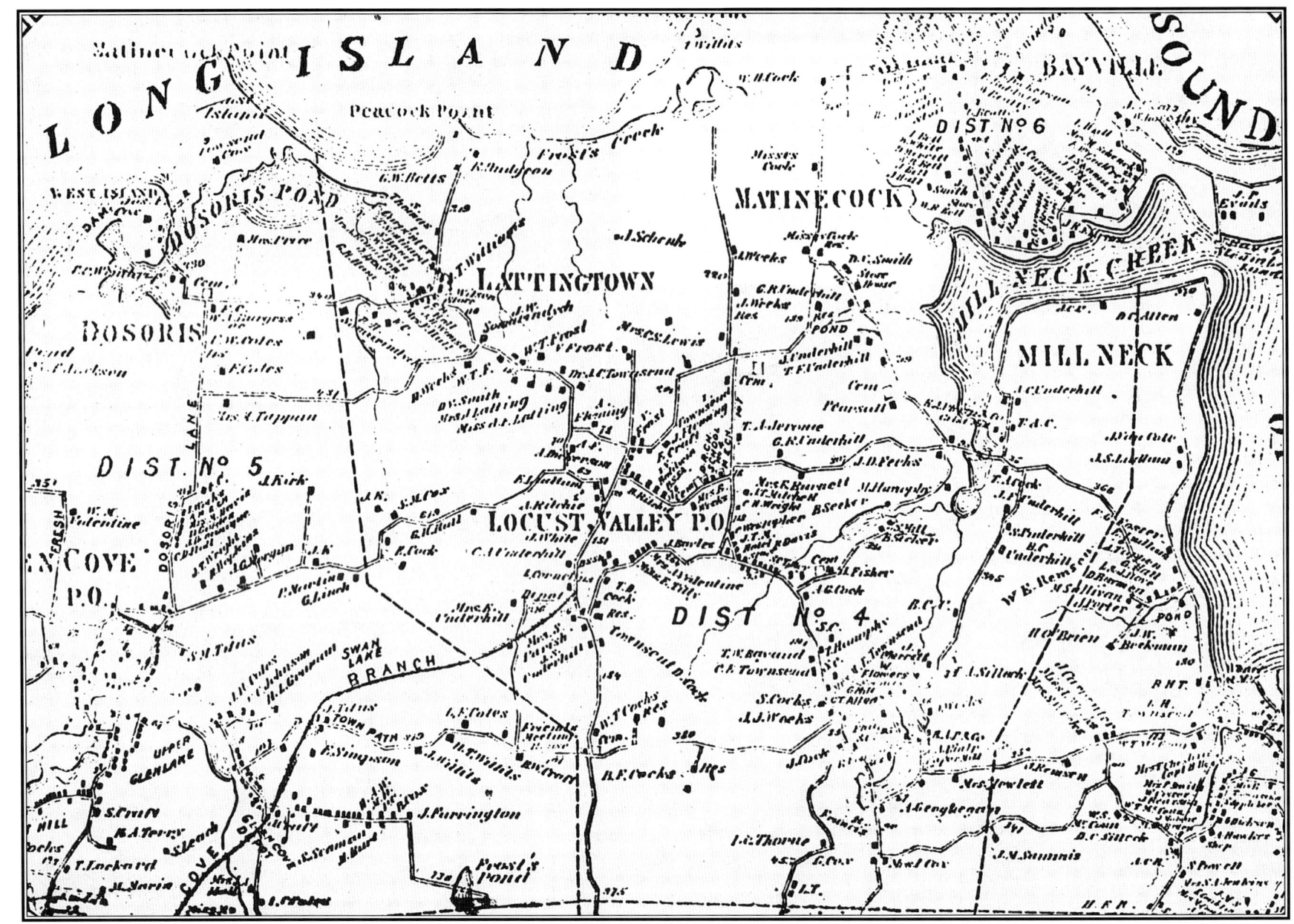

Map of the North Shore circa 1876

LEFT: The Frost cemetery

Captain John Underhill

Algonquin tribe whose name meant "the land of overlooks." After appointing him sheriff to help stop the smuggling that was rife at the time, especially at Oyster Bay and Musketa Cove (Glen Cove), Governor Nichols instructed Captain John Underhill to purchase 250 acres of land, known as Matinecock, from the Indians. In June 1667 seven Indians executed deeds for seven tracts of land to seven families of settlers, with Underhill acting as financial advisor to the Indians.

One of the settlers was William Simson, who sold his land to the Frost family in 1674. William Frost had come from New Haven to Southhold in 1655 and thence to Locust Valley in 1674, the year his friend Underhill died. The land remained in the Frost family until it was sold to Paul Cravath in 1890.

There are two cemeteries on the former Cravath property, one for the Frost family, with gravestones dating back at least to 1776, supposedly containing the unmarked grave of William Frost. The other was for slaves, who were buried in unmarked graves. The Frost cemetery is directly behind the 17th, the slave cemetery on the knoll behind the 15th green.

The area was called *Buckram* in 1730, a name that was later changed to *Locust Valley* in 1856, in recognition of the 1,700 locust trees brought to the area from Virginia by John Sands. In 1775 Sand's descendants led America's first "Declaration of Independence," that of Long Island's North Shore farmers against the Loyalist landed gentry of Hempstead.

Clarence Mackay's Harbor Hill in Roslyn
Photograph by Monica Randall

CHAPTER 2

The Gold Coast

As the nineteenth century neared its conclusion, the North Shore was simple farmland and the landholders were people who had dedicated themselves as a matter of religious principle to the most simple and frugal of lives. Many were Quakers; their ancestors had come across the Sound from Stamford, Connecticut, nearly two hundred years before.

The Meadow Brook Hunt Club was in no small way responsible for the transformation of the North Shore. It was established in 1881 by August Belmont and his circle of friends, long before the first Gold Coast mansion was built. Soon the horse became the focal point of North Shore life, as it was of English country life.

Fox hunting flourished with great elegance on the North Shore. The men and women of nobility, clad in "pink" riding coats, engaged weekly, some almost daily, in the chase, in hot pursuit of the hounds from one estate to the next. The special meets were accompanied by hunt breakfasts and lavish balls afterwards.

The "gentlemanly" sport of polo became the ultimate status symbol, attracting spectators from across the country, even from Europe, to watch the games at Meadow Brook's fields in Old Westbury.

It was through his involvement with Meadow Brook Hunt that Charles Pratt, co-founder with John D. Rockefeller of Standard Oil, came to know the North Shore countryside, and began buying land there. By 1885 he owned more than two square miles of farmland and woodland in Glen Cove, which he called Dosoris Park.

> "It was the 'Gold Coast' when it glittered, a time of elegance and splendor, gilded ceilings, private yachts, castles surrounded by polo fields, marble pavilions, and formal gardens."
>
> —*The Mansions of Long Island's Gold Coast*

The million-dollar estate he built there, called *Killenworth,* was acclaimed as one of America's grandest homes (it is now the Russian Mission to the United Nations). Pratt built an additional eighteen homes in Dosoris Park, for each of his six sons and two daughters, as well as other relatives.

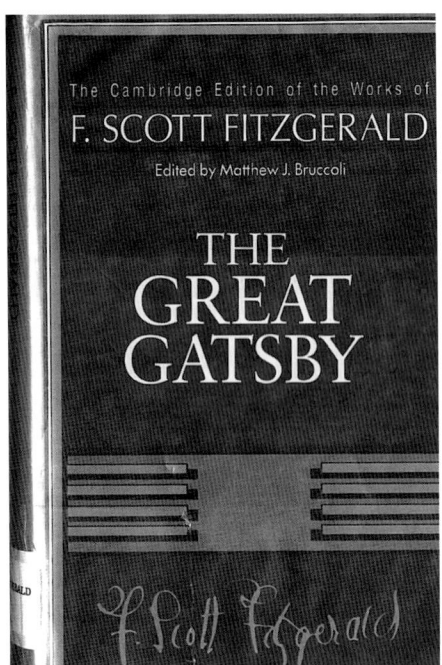

Dust cover of the *Great Gatsby*

The most impressive of the houses was the one built for son Herbert L. Pratt, which is now Webb Institute, a private school of naval architecture.

Also within the park were formal gardens, a gun club, and eventually a nine-hole golf course that would blossom as the Nassau Country Club. An indoor tennis court was an early addition, and a second one was built in 1932 at a cost of $250,000, "to help out local unemployment during the Depression."

The Pratts were the first to "discover" the North Shore. Soon others would follow, as great fortunes were made from America's growing industries, and the Gold Coast was born. During the first decade of this century, numerous castles, Italian villas, and French chateaux began to adorn the coast of Long Island Sound, from Manhasset to Huntington, landscaped with formal gardens inspired by Europe's palatial residences.

Few of the Gold Coast mansions were as dramatic as the 110-acre Old Westbury estate of noted horseman Francis P. Garvan, an assistant Attorney General of New York and renowned devotee of American decorative arts. His gabled Tudor mansion was crowned with a Victorian cupola, and a Gothic tower stood on one side.

The Gold Coast Era has been written about extensively, indeed immortalized in F. Scott Fitzgerald's classic novel, *The Great Gatsby*. We have selected two pieces here to present the flavor of the times. Our first describes the perspective of the curious outsider. It is taken from an article entitled "*Luxury Land*," which was published in the August 1948 edition of *Holiday Magazine*.

"If you drive out to the eastward over the Triborough Bridge from Manhattan you will reach the Grand Central Parkway. And after you have passed LaGuardia Field and the forlorn site of the World's Fair grounds you will presently find yourself at the juncture of three main roads: the Parkway itself, Northern Boulevard and Jericho Turnpike. Take any one of the three, let ten miles accumulate on your speedometer, turn left at the first opportunity, and you will find yourself in the midst of the North Shore.

"You can drive all day along the little roads which wind among ancient shade trees without once recrossing your trail. Occasionally you will encounter a concrete highway, but for the most part you will be deep in quiet countryside. Now and again you will go through a village—Glen Cove or East Norwich, Jericho or Roslyn, Locust Valley or Lattingtown. It will be quite an undistinguished settlement: an A&P Supermarket and a drugstore certifying its kinship with a thousand other American towns, although it may have a saddler's shop or an ancient village hall to give it some small distinction.

"You will pass emerald meadows that you will instantly identify as golf courses. You will also ride alongside endless stretches of brick wall—much of it quite handsomely laid in the serpentine fashion—and similar reaches of wattle fence or privet hedge grown ten feet high. And when your day's outing is done you probably will possess a deep sense of frustration. For with all your driving through the heart of the North Shore you will not have seen a single mansion, not even an imposing facade. You will cherish no glimpse of the happy sons and daughters of the rich taking their ease upon shaded terraces.

"This because the habit and fashion of life on the North Shore, set so long ago by Charles Pratt and followed ever since with strict devotion, is the habit and fashion of hidden and jealous privacy. It is a little odd that this should be so. For the development of the North Shore by the millionaires began at the very time when the chief idea of being a millionaire at all was to build a Show Place. It was the biggest thing a millionaire could get for his money: to hire the most expensive architects of the land, to pick a site easy of access to the multitudes, and to build a house which common folk would come from miles around to see and to covet. The Show Place was the one badge of success which could not be counterfeited."

Of the people of the Gold Coast, we present some interesting comments from Monica Randall's book, *The Mansions of Long Island's Gold Coast,* published in 1979:

"The Long Island Set, as it was known, was very much a principled world unto itself. These people lived by graceful codes of protocol, and maintained an air of decency and dignity, and if they occasionally fell from grace, the people who lived by those rules never forgot that they existed. This 'set' had, and still has, its exclusive clubs, the much coveted memberships to either The Creek, Piping Rock, or Seawanhaka Corinthian Yacht Club. Lands of members of the set were always open to their neighbors who belonged to it, and riders on horseback could find their way across much of the North Shore through the many connecting trails. It should also be noted that the caretakers, gatekeepers, and other staff who worked on an estate all their lives were allowed to remain in their often charming and rustic little estate cottages.

"It was a time of great style, where the wealthy surrounded themselves with big cars, gorgeous clothes, lots of parties and fun. A typical day on the Gold Coast would start with a game of golf on a private course, then lunch at Piping Rock Club terrace with much talk of horses, then on to the Meadowbrook Club where the game of polo came alive. With one's friends, one would fill the Rolls Royces and head for the nearest dinner party that often ended with a Charleston contest.

"The millionaires and tycoons with their newly amassed fortunes indulged their every whim in trying to outdo their friends and business rivals. Lavish parties were held.

"Endless rounds of coming-out parties were given under pink and white tents, festooned with masses of orange blossoms, fluttering ribbons and flowers draped over arcades of trellises.

"When Prohibition struck, the parties got even wilder, as stills were set up in the basements of the estates, and rum-running became the rage."

Marshall Field's estate Caumsett. Photograph by Monica Randall

The Garvan estate
Photograph by Monica Randall

Before the crash of 1929 there were over five hundred "Flapper Age" mansions on Long Island's North Shore. Fewer than half of them exist today. The glitter dimmed with the Depression. Many of the North Shore families survived the heavy taxation through intermarriages with each other, in the hope that their way of life could continue. But it became impossible to maintain the large staffs of servants needed to care for the huge homes. Many of the castles were abandoned, and ultimately torn down.

J. P. Morgan's estate in Glen Cove. Photograph by Monica Randall

ABOVE: Veraton
RIGHT: Paul Cravath

18 The Creek

CHAPTER 3

Veraton

The land our club occupies was once part of one of the Gold Coast's most magnificent estates, Veraton, the home of corporate lawyer Paul Cravath.

When Cravath first came to Locust Valley circa 1890, he bought a large piece of property that later became the village of Lattingtown. Wild and wooded, it stretched from Lattingtown Road to the Sound. What then was called the Little Meadow Brook, a branch of Frost Creek, flowed into a small pond on the property.

One of Cravath's earliest land purchases included forty acres purchased from the estate of Valentine Frost not long after his death in 1890. Valentine Frost was a direct descendant of William Frost.

Cravath's estate encompassed over six hundred acres of lawn, gardens, woodlands, farmlands, paddocks, and a small picturesque lake, with driveways winding through the woods and gardens. The entranceway, seventeen hundred feet long, leading from the main gateway of the grounds to the house, was bordered by linden trees, set seventy-five feet from row to row, lining a long stretch of cultivated lawn. The grounds surrounding the house resembled one of England's historic private parks. It was noted for its natural beauty, perfect cultivation, expansiveness, system, and order. Flowers were Cravath's passion.

Cravath's home was called Veraton, after his daughter Vera. The north side of the house looked out over a beautiful stretch of countryside rolling down to the Sound. On the north lawn was a huge, vine-covered rock; on a knoll stood a great white oak, one of the largest and most perfect on Long Island, with a spread of ninety-five feet.

Twice fire struck at Veraton, the first on April 23, 1908, leaving nothing but a mass of smouldering ruins. It was forty-five minutes before the firemen arrived on the scene, and in the meantime neighbors worked valiantly to save most of the artwork and expensive furnishings, whose value later was estimated to be $160,000. The Cravaths were not living in the house at the time.

ABOVE: Side view of the estate from the formal gardens, now the fifth fairway
BELOW: The gateposts at the entrance

Cravath's loss was covered by insurance, and he quickly rebuilt Veraton on the same site. The sixty-room, two-and-one-half story, 250-foot long brick and stucco structure was considered one of the showcase mansions on Long Island. But fire struck again on April 14, 1914. This time the servants were able to save the paintings, tapestries, and antique furniture on the first floor. In spite of the valiant efforts of the Locust Valley volunteer firemen, who struggled with primitive equipment and insufficient water supply, nothing was left but the blackened walls.

The destruction of the second fire was so shocking and disheartening to Cravath that, instead of rebuilding there, he put the property up for sale and built a new home, Still House, on Duck Pond Road in Matinecock, close by his beloved Piping Rock Club. The remains of the foundation of Veraton can be seen near the Creek's sixth tee.

Paul Drennon Cravath was born in Ohio, the son of a minister. After earning his law degree at Columbia, he became one of the world's leading corporate attorneys, heading the largest law firm in the world. He handled the legal affairs of some of the nation's largest and most important corporations, fighting the "trust busters" on their behalf.

LEFT: The Cravath stable, which became the Dormie House
BELOW: The great white oak

A huge dominant figure who stood six feet four and weighed 250 pounds, Cravath was known about Manhattan for his "massive elegance, glittering presence, and overbearing pomposity." As with most of the men who became so successful in the early part of the twentieth century, Cravath insisted on having things his own way. He believed in team play, but was always captain of the team.

To others outside his business circles, Cravath was an outgoing, pleasant man who felt a great responsibility to the community where he lived, and always found time for matters others thought less important, often enlisting his influential friends. Among his pet projects was Locust Valley's Red Barn Summer Theater, one of the first and best of its kind. He also planted the handsome trees that line Locust Valley's Weir Lane, because he wanted the road approaching his estate to please him as he drove toward home.

At about the same time Cravath bought his Locust Valley holdings, one of his law partners, William D. Guthrie, bought a large tract adjacent to Cravath's western boundary, and built a mansion called *Meudon* there. Guthrie became the first mayor of Lattingtown.

The Creek 21

The clubhouse as seen from the west end in March 1925

22 The Creek

CHAPTER 4

A Quiet Club

Like very few other clubs, The Creek is fortunate in that one of its founders, Harvey D. Gibson, later took pen in hand and wrote in some detail about the club's founding and early development. We shall quote extensively, in this chapter especially, from Gibson's account, starting with the following paragraph about the club's conception:

"It was about the year 1921 that a resident of Long Island, who was a neighbor of mine, came to my office and unfolded a dream which he had conceived of founding, a new golf club on the North Shore of Long Island. To my surprise, he stated that he had walked a great deal over the Cravath property, which was the property that Mr. Davison had purchased while I was ill with pneumonia in London in 1919, and that there was one particular part of it, the only part remaining unsold, that he thought was ideally adapted for a golf course. He was certain, he said, that a club with a membership limited to not in excess of 300 would afford those belonging to it an opportunity to play golf in beautiful surroundings without being crowded at any time, even on Saturdays, Sundays and holidays."

In 1914 the boundaries of Paul Cravath's six-hundred-acre estate extended from Long Island Sound to Lattingtown Road on the south, and between Sheep Lane on the east and the club's present western boundary. Late in 1919, Henry P. Davison put together a small syndicate (including Gibson, who was ill with pneumonia in London at the time, and unaware of the goings-on) that bought Cravath's estate. In fact, there are deeds transferring the land from Cravath to Davison, Gibson, George F. Baker, Jr., and George Galt Bourne dated January 23, 1920 (and finally filed on June 28, 1921), suggesting that these four gentlemen comprised the original syndicate.

Gibson himself then purchased a hundred acres near the water from the syndicate, and there built his mansion, Land's End, where he lived until his death in 1950. His wife continued on the estate until her death in 1974. Another 88 acres were sold to Baker. By late 1922, only 186 of the original 600 acres remained unsold, and they formed the tract destined for the new golf club.

Harvey Gibson sketched in pencil

ABOVE: The Duke and Duchess of Windsor standing in front of the Tower House
BELOW: Jim Keresey, Great Britain's Prince Andrew, and Bill Kenny (L to R) in July of 1995

Baker built a home on his property for his daughter Florence and her (first) husband, the noted amateur golfer Tommy Tailer. The Duke and Duchess of Windsor were annual guests in that house, now called the Tower House, and the Duke was a frequent golfer at The Creek. (The Duke's grand-nephew, Prince Andrew, recently visited The Creek to include the club in a BBC documentary he was doing about his famous ancestor.)

The following passage traces the club's embryonic period, from Gibson's initial skepticism about the financing of such a project to his realization that The Creek was, indeed, a distinct possibility:

"The value of the property was so great that I, at the start, rather questioned the practicability of his idea. However, he seemed to think that with existing low taxes and prosperous business that little difficulty would be encountered in arranging the required financing; and as he discussed the various aspects, it gradually sounded more and more as though it had possibilities. Without manifesting too much enthusiasm I told him that I would talk it over with some of my friends and see what they thought about it and thanked him for his interest.

"Shortly thereafter I acquainted Frank Crocker, who had been the leader in the formation of a number of important clubs, with the plan and found him enthusiastic, and he suggested that we consult and obtain the views of Charles B. Macdonald, the father of golf and the person who had laid out many of the famous golf courses in the East. Charlie Macdonald also manifested great interest and expressed a desire to go over the proposed property as promptly as possible. Within a few days the three of us with one of Mr. Macdonald's golf course engineers walked over what was to be the proposed course to visualize the layout. We were unanimous in our opinion that possibilities existed for a very fine golf course, in fact, an outstanding one."

If the above suggests fast work on Macdonald's part in coming up with a proposed layout for an 18-hole course, consider the possibility that Macdonald might have been familiar with the land. It has been said that The Creek property was one of the sites he considered, but rejected, for his National Golf Links during the first decade of the century. And it was Macdonald who built Piping Rock's course a decade earlier, at which time he no doubt made the acquaintance of Paul Cravath. Indeed, Cravath was in the forefront of the "horse set" at Piping Rock who tormented Macdonald by parading their horses across his cultivated fairways. That Macdonald may have gained his revenge by turning Cravath's estate into a golf course is as amusing as it is ironic.

The efficacy of the project, of course, hinged on the availability of the land, which at the time was controlled by the syndicate. Gibson continues his account, telling how The Creek acquired its spectacular piece of property overlooking Long Island Sound:

"Everyone of us was all for going ahead with it. My next step was to discuss the matter with Henry P. Davison, who at the time was quite ill, from which illness he did not recover. He was happy to learn that there was a possibility of the property being used in such a splendid way for the enjoyment of the surrounding community. He had for years ridden horseback over the property and had always considered it the most outstanding on Long Island. He expressed the hope that I would apply myself energetically to bring such a club into being, which I promised to do. Unfortunately, he did not live to see it a reality.

"After reporting back to Frank Crocker and Charlie Macdonald as to my conversation with Mr. Davison, we went forward and formed an organizing committee for the club, and a very distinguished one it was. The members of it were the following gentlemen: Vincent Astor, George F. Baker, Jr., Frank L. Crocker, Marshall Field, Clarence H. Mackay, Charles B. Macdonald, J. P. Morgan, Herbert L. Pratt, Harry Payne Whitney, John D. Ryan and myself. Each member of the committee approached liked the idea and agreed to serve."

The club's founding fathers, the organizing committee of eleven, was truly impressive, a "Who's Who of the Long Island Set," the elite who set the tone for the Gold Coast's high society during the Roarin' Twenties. That men of such fabulous wealth would have to think twice about financing such a project at a time of such great extravagance is difficult to fathom. We let Gibson continue with their monetary struggles:

"The next step was to make the actual plans for the course and buildings. Charlie Macdonald with his engineers busied himself with the layout of the golf course and an architectural firm went to work on the buildings. Simultaneously the organizing committee went forward with the financing. A corporation known as the Kellenworth Corporation with an initial capital of $900,000 (the equivalent of $9.8 million today) represented by three hundred shares of stock at $3,000 each was formed to take title to the property and to construct the course

The original letter soliciting membership

ABOVE: The lounge as it appeared in 1924

ABOVE RIGHT: The fireplace in the lounge, as seen in 1926

and buildings. The requisite on one becoming a member of the club was that he own one share of Kellenworth Corporation stock. A small group was formed with little difficulty to underwrite the full amount, which underwriting was to be later ratified by the purchase of stock by the individual members."

Everything seemed in place for the club's birth. However, there was one final obstacle for the new club to overcome—the presence of an unidentified dissenter in the ranks. Gibson tells us of some local opposition to the presence of the club in the community, of one of the founders' subsequent attempt in the latter half of 1922 to stop the formation of the club, and of his own steadfastness in the face of such discontent:

"These steps having been taken, work was started with the objective of getting the club ready for play as soon as possible. When the golf course had become about half constructed with the bunkers all completed and greens formed with various layers of soil in place, I was asked one day to ride to my business in New York with one of the members of our organizing committee on his yacht. He was accompanied by another gentleman who was not a member of the committee but who resided in the community. To my great surprise the member of the committee expressed himself as violently opposed to carrying the club through to completion. He was a close

26   The Creek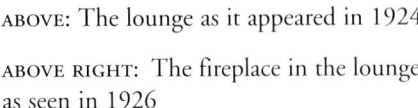

friend of the other gentleman with us, and it was obvious that he had partially at least been persuaded by his friend to take such a position. Up to then there had been no evidence of anything but enthusiasm on the part of everyone which naturally made my surprise the greater.

"They said that in their opinion the club was going to be a blot on the landscape in the exclusive community where located, and that there would be unsightly water towers constructed and all sorts of other objectionable features. They urged me to join them in their opposition. I pointed out to them that they were the first ones who had at any time raised any question about the desirability of the club; that our committee had gone forward after unanimously approving it; that the cost was all underwritten; that we had already spent $106,000 on construction and that it would certainly cost another $25,000 at least to restore the land and fill in the bunkers; and that it did not seem practical to me to change the plans, even if such procedure were generally favored and I knew of no one who had such a new idea except themselves.

"They continued, however, stoutly to maintain that the cost of abandonment of the plans, whatever it turned out to be, would be money well spent because the club would never, in their opinion, be successful; and that in any event, it was most desirable that the community be confined to residential estates.

"I reminded them that Mr. Davison had been most enthusiastic about it, and that he had passed away, with complete assurance and gratification that there was going to be a local community golf club on this property and that I for one was not going to let him down; that I could not join them in their opposition and, in fact, was going to do my very best to carry the project through to a successful conclusion.

"They seemed disappointed at their inability to convert me to their ideas. When I got to town the first thing I did was to tell Frank Crocker of the conversation. He was infuriated, and said he would go immediately to see the committee's wishes were going to prevail, which he did."

Of course, Gibson and his compatriots did prevail, and The Creek was brought into this world as planned. According to Gibson:

"Without further opposition of any sort the

The Creek

TEL.- GLEN COVE 1405
P.O.- LOCUST VALLEY

PRESIDENT
CLARENCE H. MACKAY

VICE PRESIDENTS
J. PIERPONT MORGAN
FRANK L. CROCKER

TREASURER
HARVEY D. GIBSON

SECRETARY
MARSHALL FIELD

GOVERNORS
VINCENT ASTOR — CHARLES B. MacDONALD
FRANK L. CROCKER — CLARENCE H. MACKAY
MARSHALL FIELD — J. PIERPONT MORGAN
HARVEY D. GIBSON — HERBERT L. PRATT
EDWARD S. HARKNESS — JOHN D. RYAN
RICHARD F. HOWE — HARRY PAYNE WHITNEY

TO THE MEMBERS OF THE CREEK:

THE MEN'S CLUBHOUSE AND THE GOLF COURSE WILL BE FORMALLY OPENED UPON SEPTEMBER 15TH. APPROPRIATE GOLF COMPETITIONS, NOTICE OF WHICH WILL BE GIVEN LATER, WILL BE ARRANGED BY THE GREEN COMMITTEE FOR THE WEEK FOLLOWING THE OPENING.

THE BATH HOUSES AND BATHING BEACH ARE NOW AVAILABLE FOR MEMBERS AND THEIR FAMILIES AND GUESTS.

TWELVE HOLES OF GOLF, ALTHOUGH NOT YET COMPLETED, ARE PLAYABLE AND THE PROFESSIONAL, JACK ROSS, IS IN ATTENDANCE.

AFTER AUGUST TENTH, LUNCHES AND DINNERS MAY BE OBTAINED AT THE MEN'S CLUBHOUSE UPON NOTIFYING THE STEWARD IN ADVANCE.

Marshall Field
SECRETARY.

AUGUST FIRST, 1923

List of original officers and governors and the announcement of club's opening

> *The fuss and expense of the average country club are here avoided. At the Creek, the site of a large and luxurious mansion still remains, but the organizing committee has wisely decided not to rebuild what, unfortunately for Mr. Paul Cravath, the former owner, was burned down. Instead the stables had been cunningly remodeled by Messers. Walker & Gillette into a man's locker room and lounging place, with a few modest bedrooms; while a few yards away is a Casino with dining-room and living-room where the better sex may also come. This latter commands a lovely view of the course and of Long Island Sound. And all this can be run by the proverbial (but so seldom obtainable) man and his wife. Mr. Elam and Mrs. Elam (how biblically Scotch are the names!) have for fifteen years managed the club of the Royal and Ancient at St. Andrews and are well known to American golfers. After June they will be high steward and matron of The Creek.*
>
> TOWN & COUNTRY,
> *February 1, 1923*

contemplated 300 members were procured with little difficulty and the under-writers were relieved of their initial responsibility by the purchase by each member of the required $3,000 worth of stock of the holding corporation which owned the property on which the golf course was constructed. As is generally the case in the construction of a golf course, the amount of the expected cost was exceeded making necessary placing a first mortgage of $375,000 on the property.

"The Club came into being with great enthusiasm on the part of everybody connected with its creation. It was regarded as a magnificent course and the organization committee, with one exception, and with the addition of Edward S. Harkness and Richard Howe became the original board of governors." (Astor's place of residence, incidentally, was listed as Rhinebeck, New York, and Ryan's as Butte, Montana.)

Membership on the Board was increased to fourteen early in 1926, when Herbert H. Dean and Paul G. Pennoyer were elected. Both would serve the club with distinction for a number of years.

The new club was named after Frost Creek, an inlet of Long Island Sound that was to play a significant role in the character of the first five holes on the back nine. Clarence Mackay served steadfastly as the club's first president, from 1923 until his death on November 12, 1938, and was followed, after more than two years of operating without a president, for twelve years by Gibson. Davison, sadly, died in May of 1922, and did not live to see the club become a reality. His son, Henry P. "Harry" Davison, Jr., became an active member and club president (1950–1955), as well as neighbor, living on Peacock Point, west of the club's grounds along the Beach.

Each member of the organizing committee was granted an "extra membership" for a personal acquaintance. Harvey Gibson used his for Artemus Gates, who would become a prominent member of the Board and club president from 1955 to 1960.

George F. Baker, Jr., a member of the original syndicate that purchased the Cravath estate, was the one member of the organizing committee not to become a member of the first Board of Governors. His son, George F. Baker III, did become a member, indeed club president from 1970 to 1975; he lived nearby on Centre Island. His mother continued to live on her estate, Vikings' Cove, west of the club, until her death in 1977.

The initial cost of the club was $1,002,000. To secure this amount the Kellenworth Corporation sold Kellenworth stock to members in the amount of $627,000 and borrowed $375,000 from New York Trust Company on a first mortgage covering all of the land, buildings, and improvements of the club. In the first few years after the club was started, additional improvements and facilities had been added at the further cost of approximately half a million dollars, paid for by additional sales of Kellenworth stock and gifts by members.

The premises were leased by the Kellenworth Corporation to The Creek for a term of ninety-nine years. The lease called for The Creek to pay Kellenworth a yearly rental in an amount equal to the fixed charges to the Corporation covering interest and amortization on the mortgage, taxes, and insurance.

When reporting on the club's incorporation in its January 20 edition, the *New York Times* dubbed The Creek the "Million Dollar Golf Club," asserting that it was "undoubtedly the richest golf club in the world." The reporter also claimed the golf course to be "unique, the finest golf course in the country, if not the world."

The club's purpose, according to its constitution, was to "further social and sporting activities, and to provide a relaxed atmosphere in which to enjoy golf and fine food." The legal document incorporating "The Creek, Inc." dated January 12, 1923, stated the club's "raison d'être" more formally:

"The particular objects for which this corporation is being formed are: to provide and maintain a golf course, tennis courts, bathing beach, and other facilities for out-of-door recreation and sport, and to conduct and operate a social club for the benefit of its members."

The club's Bylaws, adopted at the first Board meeting on June 11, 1923, stipulated that operating expenses were to be divided equally among the members, the payment of which would be considered their dues, payable semi-annually based on the club's budget. There would be no initiation fee.

The Rules of the club, also adopted at that June 11 meeting, forbade the staff from possessing or handling any bottles containing alcoholic liquors on the premises, even if requested by the members. In 1926, the House Committee formally requested the members and staff to abide by the Volstead Act (Prohibition). Several committees were appointed at that first Board meeting, including the Green Committee (Macdonald as chair, Pratt, and Whitney), the House Committee (Gibson as chair, Charles L. Tiffany, and Mrs. A. Stewart Walker), as well as the Membership Committee. It was also agreed

Scenes inside the Dormie House circa 1924.
LEFT: The lounge
ABOVE: The Tap Room
BELOW: The locker room

The back of the Dormie House and first tee in 1924

> "Few clubs in this country, in fact, I might say, no other club in this country can boast of such a membership, including as it does men whose names are prominent in every walk of life and who are in many ways important factors in the phases of life they are connected with. These men, having large estates in the fashionable country home section on or near the north shore, organized this club and limited its membership to two hundred as a means of offsetting the ever increasing congestion of the other courses on which they played. In other words, they will have golf as they desire to play it within easy access of their palatial homes.
>
> "Members and their guests who arrive at The Creek by water did not have to lose any time in starting. The tenth hole is located on the shore of Long Island Sound, and players are permitted to cut in there. Incidentally, players may also pause here on their way from the ninth green to take a dip before they tackle the back nine, for there is a bathing pavilion close at hand."
>
> *Golf Illustrated*
> August 1924

to limit the membership to two hundred initially to see how that worked out, perhaps hoping to emulate such exclusive, small membership clubs as Old Elm, Blind Brook, The Links, and Pine Valley.

The club's brick colonial buildings, the Casino, Dormie House, and Beach House, all were designed by Walker & Gillette. The Casino (now referred to as the *Main Clubhouse*) was furnished in Georgian Greek Renaissance style, and featured a lounge, the east end of which was used for dining, the center portion as a lounge or for dancing, and the western end as a formal living room. An outside terrace overlooking the Sound and the distant shores of Connecticut, was to be used for dining in the warmer months. The building included a pair of second-floor bedrooms on either end, each pair sharing a common bathroom. The kitchen was located in the basement.

What once had been a stable on the Cravath estate was converted into the Dormie House, a male retreat that included two locker rooms, lounge, tap room, kitchen, and the pro shop, with dormitory space upstairs. The original lockers were paneled, set above an upholstered seat, under which was a locked drawer for smaller possessions.

The original Cravath mansion was located between the clubhouse and the sixth tee, where the remains of the foundation can be seen. It was thought originally that the Casino would be built on this site.

The Dormie House, Beach House, and bathing beach opened on September 15, 1923, along with twelve holes of the golf course, which were playable although not yet completed. The Casino was unveiled the following Spring.

The club's operating costs were reduced significantly that first season as a result of the many gifts to the club by the members, such items as china and silverware, for example, and other furnishings for the two buildings, as well as $7,500 in cash. Francis P. Garvan "loaned" the club the early American furniture that adorned the Casino, and E. F. Hutton donated some of the furnishings. J. Vincent Astor donated a permanent pier for the Beach.

During the early years, the club's budget provided for a working fund to cover such items as cuisine, cigars, playing cards, coal, and stationery.

At a meeting before the start of the 1924 season, when it was decided to limit use of the Dormie House to men, with some special exceptions decided by the House Committee, it was also decided to drop the term "Casino" from the club's lexicon, the main building to be known thereafter as the *Club House*. The members were able to hold private "entertainments" in the Club House, the Dormie House, and the Beach House.

Following the 1925 season, the ban against women in the Dormie House was lifted, and although a women's locker room there was proposed in 1926, that idea was tabled, to be implemented in the late 1920s.

Although a committee was appointed in 1923, chaired by Clarence Mackay, to plan for a formal "opening day," ultimately it was decided to hold nothing more elaborate than a golf competition on June 3, 1924, for a "Founders Cup" donated by Charles Blair Macdonald.

On January 15, 1927, the newly appointed tennis committee recommended two en-tout-cas courts, to be built on one of two possible locations. Their preference was an area near the second green, quite possibly the present site of the paddle courts, while their second choice was in the old garden near the fifth green. The Board approved the latter site, where the two courts were built. Artemus Gates served as the club's first Tennis chairman, and Mrs. Kenneth O'Brien, Jr., volunteered to raise the $7,500 to pay for the courts. Her husband, along with Clarence Mackay and J. P. Morgan, was among her primary contributors. Marty Halverson was hired as the club's first tennis pro starting with the 1928 season, and he held that position through 1943.

ABOVE: An east end view of the clubhouse as it appeared in 1925

ABOVE LEFT: A bedroom in the Main Clubhouse

Cravath's Reaction

Harvey Gibson reports one final anecdote concerning Paul Cravath's reaction to the ultimate use of his old homestead:

"The architects had done such a beautiful job in remodeling the barn into a Dormie House that when at the opening of the Club and the picture of the building appeared in the daily press, Mr. Cravath, who had originally built it, remarked to Mrs. Cravath: 'Why in the world can't I ever find an architect that can build for me an attractive building like that.'"

CHAPTER 5

Titans

Many early American golf and country clubs asserted that their founding fathers, or membership in general, represented a virtual *"Who's Who In America."* No other club had a more legitimate claim of such distinction than The Creek. Many of the eleven men who founded our club were sons or grandsons of the very titans who made American finance, industry, and society what it was by the time the 1920s dawned.

Charles Blair Macdonald was a stockbroker known as a daring speculator of sizable amounts of money. Moreover, Macdonald looked upon himself as "Mr. American Golf," the man chosen as if by divine edict to supervise and govern the growth of the game in the United States. Macdonald was a big man, stubborn and humorless, with an ego to match his stature. On the other hand, he was an intelligent, articulate man, and a stickler for the Rules of golf. Above all else, he was devoted to St. Andrews and everything the Royal & Ancient represented in golf.

Macdonald's father, a wealthy man of Scottish descent, sent his son from Chicago to Scotland to be educated at St. Andrews University. Macdonald, who was born in Niagara Falls, Canada, in 1856, developed into a fine golfer during his college years, one capable of playing on nearly equal terms with the leading players of the day. But upon graduation, he returned to a golfless United States, a time in his life he described as the "dark ages."

Eventually, Macdonald built a nine-hole course for the fledgling Chicago Golf Club, which he expanded to eighteen holes in 1893, making it the first eighteen-hole course in this country.

As a golfer who finished second in two 1894 tournaments advertised as "national championships," Macdonald proved to be a quite vociferous loser, protesting among other things that an individual club had no right to conduct a national championship. As a result, Macdonald was inadvertently quite influential in the formation of the

United States Golf Association late in 1894, and won the first official U.S. Amateur Championship the following year.

Golf architecture was an avocation of Macdonald's, and he often dreamed of building a "classical" course in this country. Long Island, he always felt, was the ideal location. In 1900 his business interests brought him to Wall Street. The die was cast.

In 1901 Macdonald conceived the idea of "transatlantic translation," whereby he would build a course in this country including holes that, if not direct copies, at least embodied the principles of the great holes abroad. Macdonald wanted to "build a course that would serve as an incentive to the elevation of the game in America."

After traveling abroad in 1902, then again in 1904 and 1906, soliciting reactions and suggestions from leading figures in the game, Macdonald returned with surveyor's maps and sketches of the great holes, and interesting features of others. His plan reached fruition, with the help of engineer Seth Raynor, as the National Golf Links of America in Southampton.

That course had an enormous influence on American golf architecture. It was not an uncommon sight to see delegates from other clubs studying the National, taking voluminous notes which they would bring back home to aid their own architect build or revise their course. Macdonald, through his engineer Raynor and the latter's disciple, Charles Banks, spawned a school of golf architecture that has produced many of the finest courses in America, The Creek among them.

Clarence B. Mackay had the most colorful background of The Creek's founders. His wealth came from the California Gold Rush, where his father, John W. Mackay, an Irish immigrant (and former shipyard worker in Dublin), made a colossal fortune mining (gold and silver) the famous Comstock Lode, which he discovered. He used his fortune to found cable and telegraph companies, which his son was groomed to lead. The younger Mackay was considered one of the hardest workers among America's millionaires. Their Postal Telegraph Cable Company, which laid telegraph cables across both the Atlantic and Pacific, eventually was merged into IT&T. The Mackays also were involved in the early stages of radio communication.

Born in San Francisco in 1874, Clarence Mackay was educated in France and England, and became a benefactor of music and the fine arts. His collection of medieval armor was considered one of the greatest private collections in the world. Mackay was one of the leading Catholic laymen in the United States, and received the highest papal honors. His first wife was a suffrage leader, writer, and leading society matron; his second wife was a soprano with the Metropolitan Opera. His daughter Ellen was married to songwriter Irving Berlin.

Mackay belonged to many golf, yachting, and social clubs, among them Piping Rock, Meadow Brook, National, Nassau, Deepdale, Links, New

Mr. and Mrs. Marshall Field, on their honeymoon in 1930

The Twenties' Finest Hour

"It was here at Clarence H. Mackay's six-hundred-acre estate that one of the most fabulous parties ever given in American history took place in the summer of 1924. Upon arriving in this country to attend the international polo matches between Great Britain and the United States in Old Westbury, the Prince of Wales is quoted as having said, 'I am very impressed by the grand scale of hospitality on Long Island.'

"Grand scale indeed it was. On September 6, 1924, the handsome Prince was honored at Harbor Hill. The French chateau lit up the summer night sky in a blaze of light. There are some who say it could be seen glowing off in the distance from as far away as Connecticut. Thousands of blue electric lights glowed in the double rows of maple trees lining the mile-long drive, while towering high above the gabled roof were the stars and stripes of the American flag, especially made in electric lights for the gala occasion. Twelve hundred bejeweled guests, among them the most noted people of their time, included members of the British and American polo teams, ambassadors, brigadier generals, celebrities, nobility, and of course the fabulously rich Long Island set, all of whom had comparable show places on the Sound.

"Flowers were in abundance everywhere, while guests feasted on every conceivable culinary delight including a six foot high lobster tree set on a table in the large marquee that had been built on the lawn. A famous silver set was used for the dinner. Designed by Tiffany and Co., it was made from silver from John W. Mackay's Nevada silver mines. Scenes from the pioneer days of the Golden West were depicted. On the tables there were red roses arranged in perfect order, tied with satin ribbons, and frozen by some mysterious means in the center of huge three-hundred-pound blocks of ice. In the garden the fountains, rivaling those at Versailles, were filled with perfumed water to intoxicate the summer air, while pastel lights reflected the marble nymphs who gazed down in wonderment. Paul Whiteman and two orchestras in white tie and tails played till dawn as was the custom of the day, and there were Broadway stars to brighten the evening's entertainment. Of course, there were always those who found their way fully clothed to the bottom of the pool; footmen were on hand to fish them out and escort them upstairs to dry off."

The Mansions of Long Island's Gold Coast

Clarence Mackay

J. P. Morgan

York Yacht, Seawanhaka-Corinthian Yacht, Union League, Army & Navy, and Westminster Kennel.

Mackay's Roslyn Harbor estate, Harbor Hill, was a wedding gift from his father. It cost $6 million to build, and was a copy of the renowned French Chateau, Maison Lafitte. It was located on the highest point on Long Island, where bonfires had been built during the Revolutionary War to warn of the approach of British troops.

John D. Ryan, who was born in Michigan in 1864, became a pioneer in both copper mining and the electrification of railroads, and became the chief executive in the Anaconda Copper Mining Company. During World War I, he stepped down from managing this $700 million concern to serve as Assistant Secretary of War under Woodrow Wilson, his primary concern being the production of airplanes. This leading financier and industrialist also gave considerable time to the Red Cross during the war years. Like Mackay, Ryan was a pillar of the Catholic Church, and was honored for his work by the Pope.

Herbert Lee Pratt was born in Brooklyn in 1871, and later graduated from Amherst in 1895, a classmate of Calvin Coolidge. His father, Charles Pratt, was an associate of John D. Rockefeller, and cofounder of Standard Oil. The Pratt family later held the largest block of Standard Oil stock. Herbert Pratt eventually became president of Standard Oil; his fortune approached $10 million. The Pratts, Charles, his six sons, and two daughters, lived in separate mansions on the eight-hundred-acre family compound called Dosoris Park in Glen Cove.

Harry Payne Whitney was one of the leading figures in the history of American polo, a member of polo's "Big Four" who won the International Polo Cup in 1909, the first American victory in many years. Whitney was one of the very few men in history to hold the maximum handicap of ten goals. He also operated an imposing thoroughbred racing stable, his top horses including Irish Lad, Whiskery, and Regret, she being the first filly to win the Kentucky Derby (in 1913). Whitney helped govern both polo and thoroughbred racing.

Whitney was born in New York City in 1872, the son of William C. Whitney, former Secretary of the Navy, who made his fortune amalgamating railroads. His son was a member of the Yale class of 1894, and two years after graduation married Gertrude Vanderbilt, a noted heiress and sculptress who established the Whitney Museum of American Art. Together they amassed one of the largest fortunes in the country, and had a home on Fifth Avenue and a country home in Old Westbury that sprawled over a thousand acres, with five miles of bridle paths stretching between Post Road and Northern Blvd. The main house, later the residence of his son, Cornelius Vanderbilt Whitney, was built on the third highest point on Long Island. It was a Georgian brick manor with six white pillars overlooking what would become the Old Westbury Golf & Country Club course that today takes up just a small portion of the original estate. There, Whitney earned a reputation for his entertainments. He also was a dog fancier and enthusiastic yachtsman.

Frank Longfellow Crocker, a descendant of poet Henry Wadsworth Longfellow, was born in Maine in 1876, was a member of the Harvard class of 1898, and obtained his law degree from N.Y.U. He became the business and legal advisor to H. P. Whitney, and was among the founders of the Whitney Museum of American Art. He also was one of the founding fathers of the Piping Rock Club, which he served as secretary for seventeen years. Crocker also assisted Macdonald in the founding of the National Golf Links in Southampton, and later of the Links Club in Manhattan and its affiliated golf club in Searingtown.

Financier Harvey Dow Gibson was born in New Hampshire in 1882, "on the wrong side of the tracks." Following graduation from Bowdoin in 1902, he went to work as a sweeper for American Express (responsible for making sure there was no uninvested cash on hand in clients' accounts). His meteoric career in the banking business culminated in 1917 when he was appointed president of Manufacturers Trust at the age of thirty-seven. Gibson worked tirelessly on behalf of the Red Cross during both world wars, and during the Depression chaired the Emergency Unemployment Relief Committee, which raised $18 million to provide food, jobs, clothing, and shelter for the needy. On the lighter side, Gibson played the banjo "professionally," and he developed one of the first ski resorts in the Northeast in his home town of North Conway, New Hampshire.

Charter member William G. Rabe was a banker who served as Harvey Gibson's personal secretary, and worked closely with C. B. Macdonald on the planning and construction of the Creek course. Rabe resided at The Creek until his death in 1987.

William Vincent Astor was born in New York in 1891, and inherited the family fortune of $87 million at age twenty-one in 1912 while a student at Harvard when his father, John Jacob Astor II, died on the *Titanic*. The family patriarch, John Jacob Astor I, the son of a butcher, came to the United States from Germany in 1783. Taking full advantage of the Louisiana Purchase, he turned a fur trading business (and some Manhattan real estate holdings) into a $20 million fortune, retiring in 1834 by far the richest man in America. His descendents used their money to develop America's railroad and shipping networks. Vincent Astor's grandmother was America's "social empress," and established the "elite 18" in 1890.

Marshall Field III was the third-generation heir to the multi-million-dollar Chicago mercantile fortune that bore his grandfather's name. Marshall Field I was a Chicago merchant and real estate man, founder of the *Chicago Sun* and Field Enterprises, a holding company for publishing enterprises, and owner of the publishing house, Simon & Shuster. His grandson, born in Chicago in 1893 and educated at Eton College of Cambridge University, earned the Silver Star while serving with the artillery in France during World War I. He later became a strong advocate of liberal causes, including the improvement of race relations, during the New Deal era.

Field spent a good deal of his early life in

Mr. and Mrs. W. Vincent Astor

England before purchasing 1,750 acres in Lloyd's Neck where he built his estate, Caumsett, in 1922, the name being a Matinecock Indian word. Field was a hospitable and gracious host, and many grand and colorful parties were staged on the extensive lawns of Caumsett for his often famous guests.

George Fisher Baker, Jr., was known in New York banking circles as "Young Mr. Baker." His father was considered the "colossus of the financial world," amassing a fortune worth $150 million, and established the First National Bank of New York, the "Bankers' Bank" (now called *Citibank*) of which his son, born in New York in 1878, became president. Young Baker and J. P. Morgan II helped stabilize the stock market following the crash of 1929, by which time his bank had become the second largest commercial bank in the world.

Baker lived on an estate near the Creek property. The Duke and Duchess of Windsor were his annual guests there (and later in the Tower House), bringing with them their own cook, valet, maid, and chauffeur. Baker was an enthusiastic yachtsman, and owned five yachts.

John Pierpoint Morgan, the son of the financier of the same name, was born in Irvington, New York, in 1867. His father, a New York banker and international financier, founded the "House of Morgan," a private banking house located at the corner of Wall and Broad Streets.

As the financier and effectively real owner of the *Titanic,* the elder Morgan was nevertheless a last-minute cancellation from the ill-fated boat's maiden voyage. Morgan died in 1913, but his bank financed loans amounting to nearly $15 billion that helped the Allies bankroll World War I.

The younger Morgan shunned publicity. In 1909 he purchased East Island and Dosoris Pond north of Glen Cove, where he developed a palatial estate known as Matinecock Point. It consisted of 110 acres and included a large pond of equal size. One had to cross a medieval-style stone bridge, complete with a 24-hour guard, who stood watch in a small guard house overlooking the churning water. Not even this prevented an assassination attempt, from which Morgan recovered. Morgan loved flowers, and won ribbons for the violets and tulips he raised. To simplify tending the garden, Morgan had a herd of cows to "mow" the front lawn.

Morgan is remembered for his philanthropic activities and his art collection, which is housed in a wing at the Metropolitan Museum of Art. He was an avid yachtsman who commuted to his Wall Street offices each day on a small steam powered boat called the Nevett, that carried a crew of ten men. Morgan belonged to several yacht clubs, and his best-known yacht was the Corsair.

Paul G. Pennoyer, a prominent Board member during the club's early years, was Morgan's son-in-law. Herbert Hollingshead Dean, destined to become C. B. Macdonald's antagonist regarding the golf course, was a banker and member of the New York Stock Exchange.

Henry Pomeroy Davison, one of the four-man syndicate that originally purchased the land that would become The Creek, died in 1922 before the club became a reality, but his son, H.

George Baker

Member H. H. Ramsey, USGA president 1931–1932

P. "Harry" Davison, Jr., did become a prominent member. Both father and son were lifelong bankers, partners in J. P. Morgan & Company.

The elder Davison was born in Pennsylvania in 1867. Educated at several Ivy League schools, he quickly rose from teller/cashier to become president of First National Bank before joining Morgan. A beloved financier, benefactor of the needy, he was active worldwide with the Red Cross during World War I. His son, born in Englewood, New Jersey, in 1898, took a leave from Yale to become a naval aviator in that war, then returned to get his degree in 1920. He then joined Morgan after a year abroad at Cambridge.

Like his neighbor, Paul Cravath, Davison's mansion on Peacock Point burned to the ground, one year before the second Veraton fire.

George Galt Bourne, also one of the original four syndicate members, was a popular figure in international society, a prototype of Gatsby era society. His father amassed the family fortune as head of the Singer Sewing Machine Company.

Edward Stephen Harkness was the ultimate anonymous philanthropist. His father amassed a vast fortune as an early partner of John D. Rockefeller. The son, who was born in Cleveland, Ohio, in 1874, donated $100 million to educational and social welfare causes.

Harkness graduated as a member of the Yale class of 1897 before studying law at St. Andrews University in Scotland and earning his law degree from Columbia. He became a railway financier, director of the Southern Pacific Railroad. Golf was his chief recreation, and he became a yachting advocate.

Richard Flint Howe was born in Green Bay, Wisconsin, in 1863, and graduated from Harvard in 1884. He started his career in manufacturing with International Harvester, then became a successful banker. He was an early president of The Links Club.

Herbert H. Ramsay, president of the United States Golf Association from 1931 to 1932, was a man "possessing high principles and determination," according to *Golf Illustrated*. Ramsay was a member of both Creek and National.

Edward Francis Hutton, founder in 1904 of the brokerage firm bearing his name, was born and educated in New York City. A "grease monkey" at fifteen, he quickly rose to become a partner in a brokerage firm at age twenty. He later helped organize the merger forming General Foods, and served that corporation as chairman.

ABOVE: Polo's "Big Four": Devereux Milbrun, H. P. Whitney, Monty, and Larry Waterbury

Harry Payne Whitney

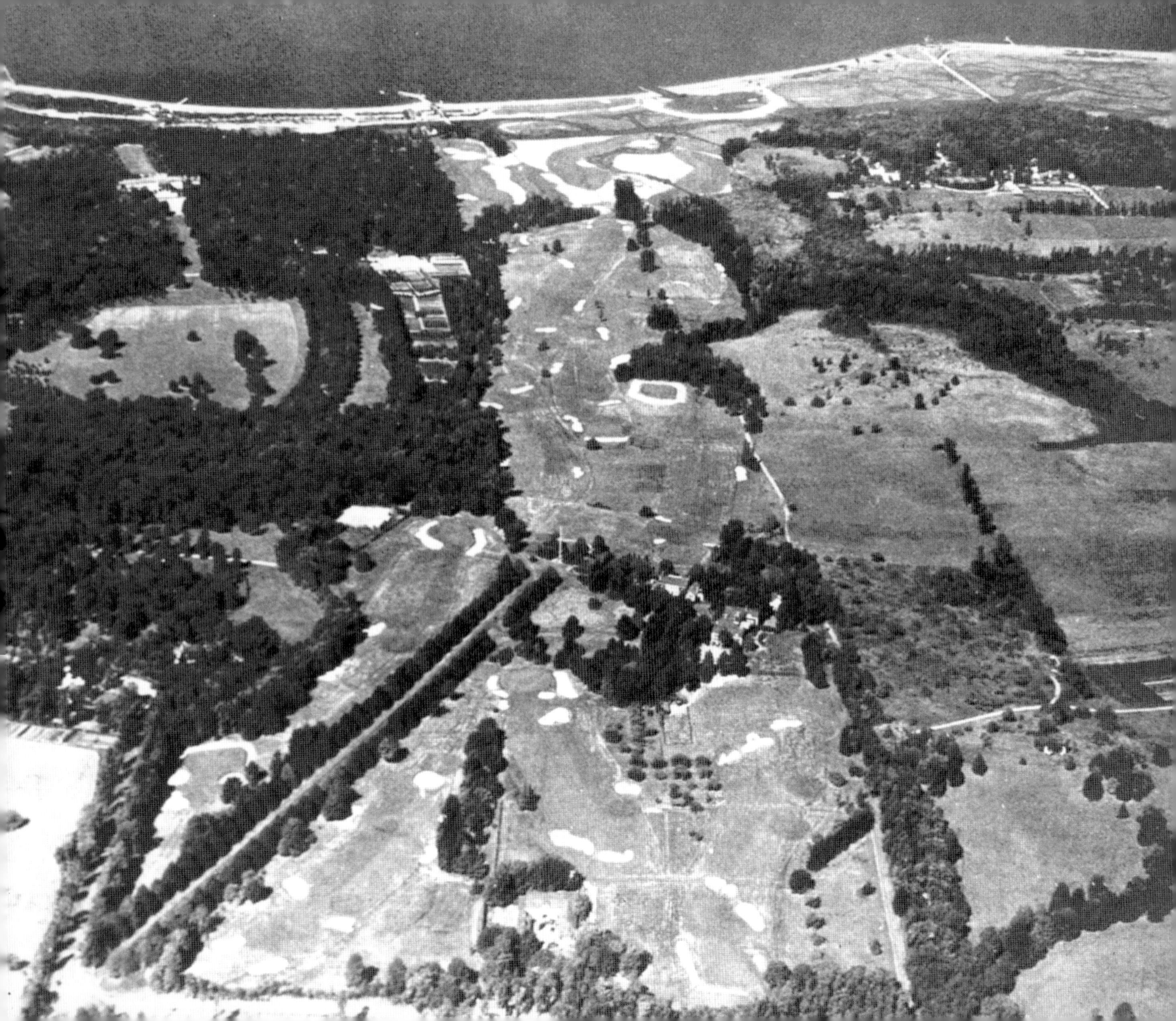

CHAPTER 6

A Macdonald Golf Course

Charles Blair Macdonald's course at The Creek was built by Seth Raynor, who was aided by Alex Balfour of Carnoustie. Raynor was Macdonald's engineer on all of his course designs starting with the National, and built a number of outstanding courses on his own as well. Macdonald, actually, was involved in the design of very few courses, the most significant in the New York area being National, Piping Rock, Sleepy Hollow, and the original Lido course, which was considered an engineering marvel, built on land reclaimed from the sea at Long Beach Island. The magnificent Lido course was rated among the three finest in the United States, along with Pine Valley and National, before its demise following World War II.

The Creek offers golfers the "best of both worlds," possessing a mix of parkland holes and seaside links. The first five holes play through tall stands of trees in what was called the "Parade Grounds," and the first five on the back nine are dominated by water, reeds, and sand-based rough. The other eight holes are quite rolling, with a scattering of trees.

When the course opened, it played to a par of 70 at 6,175 yards. Par was soon changed to 71, then dropped back to 69 when a couple of the shorter par 5s were redesignated par 4s.

The course has changed little since its inception, the major revisions involving the bunkering. William Flynn, whose credits include the present course at Shinnecock Hills and revisions at Merion and The Country Club, replaced some of Macdonald's deep bunkers below green level with sand-faced bunkers rising to green level. These have now been eliminated and converted back to the original Macdonald style.

All courses of the Macdonald-Raynor genre share certain characteristics, such as large, nearly-square greens with bold contours, often two, even three tiers, and exceptionally large and deep-faced greenside bunkers, with grassy faces and sand at ground level.

We quote Macdonald's own thoughts on greens from his book, *"Scotland's Gift: Golf"*:

"Putting greens to a golf course are what the face is to a portrait. The clothes the subject wears,

FACING PAGE: Aerial view of the golf course in 1933

> *The Courses of
> Charles Blair Macdonald*
>
> Chicago Golf Club
> National Golf Links of America
> Sleepy Hollow Country Club
> Piping Rock Club
> Lido Country Club
> The Links Club
> The Creek
> St. Louis Country Club
> Mid-Ocean Club
> The Greenbrier Hotel (Old White Course)
> Yale University Golf Course

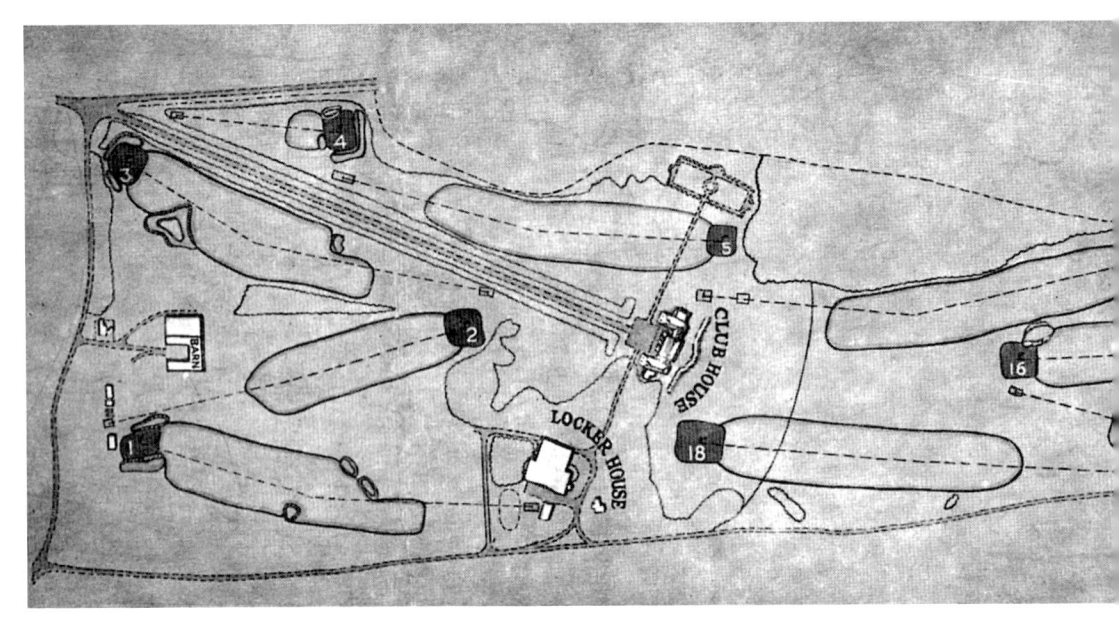

CENTER: Diagram of the golf course as originally designed

the background, whether scenery or draperies—are simply accessories; the face tells the story and determines the character and quality of the portrait."

Macdonald used fairway bunkers to present the golfer with alternate routes to the hole. His cross bunkers were placed to entice the better player to attempt a long carry from the tee to set up an easier approach to the green, while providing lesser players with an alternate route around the hazard.

The par threes typically are a "Short," an "Eden," a "Redan," and a "Biarritz," in order of increasing length, and The Creek course has one of each.

"Short" is a par three with a green encircled by bunkers and a horseshoe-shaped ridge curving through the center of the putting surface. National's sixth hole is the model; The Creek's 17th a fine example.

"Eden" is a replication of the famous 11th hole at St. Andrews in Scotland, its teardrop-shaped green guarded by a bunker at the right front ("Strath") working in tandem with a left-side bunker ("Hill"), the interplay accentuated by a back-to-front sloping green. The player avoiding the treacherous "Strath" may find his ball in "Hill," then watch an overly-aggressive recovery slip off the green—into "Strath." National's 13th is the first American copy, Creek's fourth a later rendition, and the Tillinghast green complex concept, so dramatically embodied at Winged Foot, is a spinoff. The real teeth of the Eden is the tilt of the green, fifteen feet from back to front at St. Andrews. Macdonald never tried to build as much slope into any of his Eden greens.

The "Redan" is perhaps the most dramatic of Macdonald's par threes, its front-to-back green falling away from the shot, while usually angled right-to-left (Creek's eighth hole moves left to right) behind a huge, deep bunker, which usually has a mate hidden behind the green. Our eighth hole is rather mild by "Redan" standards, when compared with National's fourth or Piping Rock's third, for example.

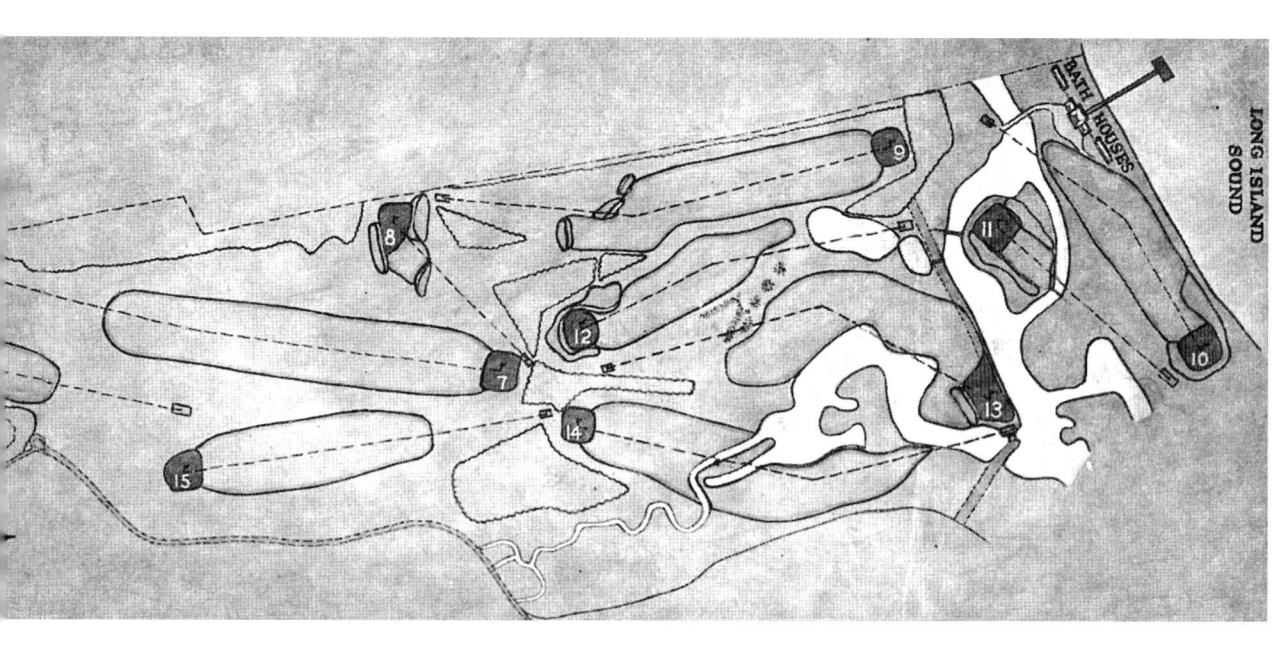

Last and longest of Macdonald's foursome of short holes, the "Biarritz" was unveiled as Piping Rock's ninth before reaching its zenith as Yale's ninth. It features an elongated green with a deep swale through the middle, as well as a pair of long thin bunkers on each side of the dance floor. In many replications, The Creek's 11th (until recently) being one, the swale precedes the green, separating the putting surface from a fairway out front. The swale at The Creek's Biarritz was originally much deeper than now, but tended to fill with water, and so the effect was softened.

The Creek's tenth hole is a prime example of Macdonald's "Cape" hole, which tempts the golfer to cut off as much of a hazard as he dares, to set up an easier approach shot. The first Cape was National's 14th, its most discussed and photographed embodiment, the fifth at Mid-Ocean.

Two other Macdonald trademarks very much in evidence at National appear to have been incorporated in The Creek's dramatic sixth hole. One is the "echelon" bunker complex to be carried—or circumvented—on the tee shot, again offering the golfer the challenge of biting off as much as he dares. As the *Town & Country* article below reveals, such a bunker complex did exist in the original configuration of our sixth hole, and an aerial map from 1933 shows crossbunkers at the first, second, and fifth holes. Almost every Macdonald-Raynor course has a punchbowl green, some completely hidden, others angled, as is our sixth.

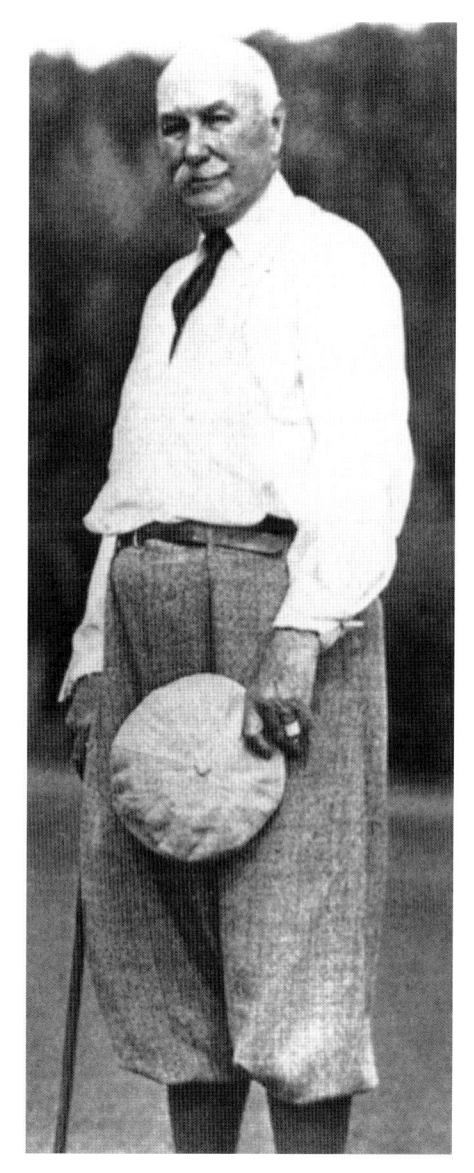

Charles Blair Macdonald

The Creek 43

Seth Raynor

"As for the course, it stretches like a green carpet, falling in gentle folds from the terrace of the old Cravath place right down to the Sound. And the player on the tee of the sixth hole will stand as on a peak in Darien and may look away down to the beach where the yachts lie at anchor by the ninth hole, and across the Sound to the bright Connecticut shore. Or he may gaze more closely with a wild surmise at the bunker in front of him and down steeply to the Punch Bowl, just 420 yards away, and see his golfing future mapped out before him, either hideous ruin or a perfect par four. Mr. Raynor, who laid out the course, says there is a hole like this at Mountain Lake in Florida. Doubtless he knows. But we can think of no hole so spectacular in point of landscape and golfing beauty in Northern climes.

"Next, perhaps, in quality comes the tenth hole, which lies along the salt water's edge, like the eighth at the Lido. This hole takes after the seventeenth at the National, only the long carry is on the right and the big sand dune which takes the place of the hummocks covers the left half of the green. In other words, it is the seventeenth reversed. Also it includes a water carry. Indeed, there are many water hazards at this end of the course. Here the sea meadows have been dredged and are now contained by a dyke and are still, like Holland, a foot or more below high tide. Mr. Raynor, who, with Mr. Charles Macdonald's advice, made the course, has laid out in this space five of the most original water holes in existence. The eleventh, or Biarritz hole, like the ninth at Piping Rock, has the added feature of a water carry of 150 yards. The thirteenth and fourteenth are both entirely original holes the thirteenth being of a decided dogleg variety and the fourteenth curving a little across two water hazards. The Creek is not a dry course. On the other hand, the greens for the most part stand up boldly and defiantly, daring the player to come on and take his chances. From at least eleven greens the view expands away over the Sound. Mr. Raynor has worked with enthusiasm and an eye for detail as well as for broad effect. He rightly points out the merit of the tenth hole along the Sound which points northeast, so that there is never a glare of sun off the water in the face of the player. Very few water holes can say as much."

Town & Country
February 1, 1923

The "St. Andrews swing" of British champion Cecil Leitch from what is thought to be our sixth tee, with the fifth green in background

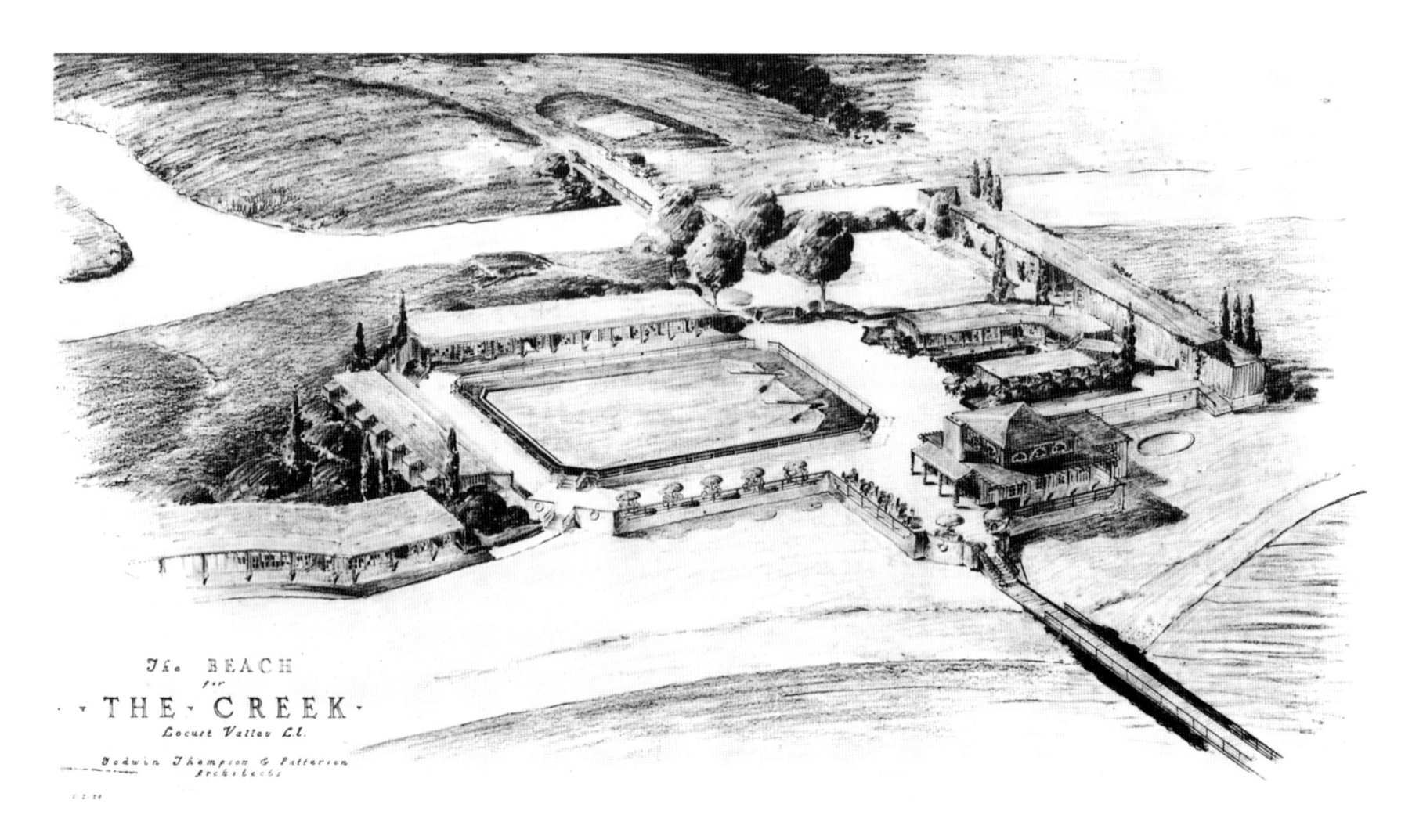

Architect's sketch of the Beach and yacht landing

CHAPTER 7

The Beach

The Creek is one of the few clubs in the United States to have a bathing beach (and at one time a yacht anchorage facility) on its property. On Long Island, only Maidstone in East Hampton has similar facilities. The idea, once again, came from Harvey Gibson, a few years after the club's inception. In a sense, the Beach was Gibson's "pet project," and we let him describe its evolution:

"It had always seemed to me that some special use should be made of the beach for club purposes and that it should be developed; so about three or four years after the club was opened I requested our architects to make a study and to prepare colored sketches for a contemplated development.

"The study when finished called for a large swimming pool surrounded by cabanas with a casino for restaurant service and dancing. It was the usual type of beach development such as exists at Palm Beach, Miami, and other places in the South.

"The cost was estimated to be approximately $125,000. The next question was whether any of us had enough optimism to hope that we might find some way to go forward with the project.

"The original plans called for the construction of fifty cabanas surrounding the pool and extending along the Beach. I conceived the idea of endeavoring if the governors would give the project their tentative approval on that basis, to sell the fifty cabanas to members of the club for $2,500 each. As the actual construction of the individual cabanas would cost only about $400, fifty cabanas at $2,500 each would realize the $125,000 estimated as required to carry through the whole development. The difference between the amount for which the cabanas which were to be sold and their cost would be sufficient to cover the construction of the pool and other facilities. As the ownership of a cabana entitled the member of the club purchasing it to certain rights and privileges that appeared to be most desirable, it seemed to me that there was a reasonable chance the necessary number could be sold.

"So at the next meeting of the Board of Governors of the club, which was held at the residence of Mr. J. P. Morgan, I took along the plans and drawings, purposely arriving a little ahead of

A cabana certificate of ownership dated 1931

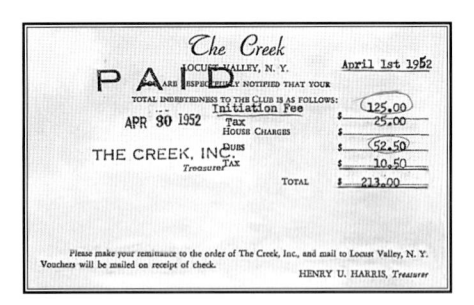

"The good old days"

time, and placed them with the colored sketch on the mantelpiece in the room where we were going to have our dinner. Mr. Morgan and I looked them over together, but I didn't tell him anything about the plan, except that it was a conception that our architects had submitted of what might be done with our waterfront property, in which I thought the Governors might be interested.

"He agreed that it presented possibilities for the distant future, but of course it was out of the question at the present time, especially with a mortgage of $375,000 outstanding against our property. As the other directors arrived for dinner, they one by one looked at the self-explanatory exhibit on the mantelpiece and turned away as a rule, with a smile and some remark to the effect that it might be something to think about twenty-five years hence. When the dinner was over, and we had finished going through our agenda, I told the Governors I would like to talk to them of my idea of selling the cabanas at $2,500 apiece and asked them if they would grant me, the Treasurer of the club, authority to go ahead with the project if I could get the whole of the cost underwritten by the advance sale of the necessary number of cabanas.

"After some discussion and a few questions, the authority requested was unanimously voted and the governors wished me luck, but ventured the opinion that they had great doubts as to whether I could sell even ten cabanas at the price contemplated.

"It turned out that they were quite wrong, because in response to a letter sent to the members of the club a few days later with which was enclosed a picture of the proposed Beach facilities, explaining that the fifty cabanas were to be sold to members at $2,500 each, and advising them as to what a cabana owner's rights would be; and also telling them that they were to be sold on a first come, first served basis, the answers came back very promptly. Within a week from the time the letters were sent out, more than the fifty available were spoken for. Among the most eager of the applicants were members of the Board of Governors of the club who only a few weeks previously had not had much faith in the success of the project. At the next following meeting of the Board the development was formally authorized and construction was started soon after.

"Very shortly thereafter it was found out that the cost was going to run over the $125,000 estimated, so we just added on eighteen more cabanas to the row on the Beach facing the Sound and sold them on the same basis as the others, thus procuring the necessary additional money.

"This Beach development, ever since it was completed some twenty-odd years ago, has been one of the most popular features of The Creek Club, outstanding, in fact, in the club life of Long Island."

To supplement Gibson's account, we note that the Board meeting at which he presented plans for the Beach took place on November 11, 1929. This is not to imply, however, that the Beach was unused until that time.

A "bath house," consisting of dressing rooms and showers, existed in 1924, if not earlier. As early as June of 1926, the club spent $2,390 to repair the bridge to the Beach, and another $1,500 to repair the road to the Beach. Club minutes of May 31, 1927 noted that the "Beach house" had opened on May 28, and that telephone service had been added. The following winter, a stone pier was built at the Beach, its $21,000 cost underwritten by member loans and a large donation from Vincent Astor.

Gibson's plans called for complementing the club's 1,200-foot Beach with a sixty-by-ninety-foot salt-water swimming pool, sixty-eight cabanas, and an attractive casino for summer dining. The original plans for the Beach House called for a large lounge in the center, with men's and women's bathhouses extending from the east and west ends of the building, and a thirty-eight-foot-long porch overlooking the Sound. Instead, a facility fairly similar to the present two-room building was constructed, with connected bath houses extending north-to-south behind the west side, inland from a wading pool, with the main pool in its present location.

The pool was unveiled on June 20, 1930, and the entire complex opened on July 1. The final cost was $165,000, leaving a reserve of nearly $5,000. Gibson was appointed the club's first Beach chairman on June 2, 1930.

The Beach looks today basically as it did in the 1930s, retaining its original character and flavor. The shells of most of the cabanas are the originals, and their rustic nature is both appealing and distinctive, a true asset to the club.

Many of the cabanas were badly damaged by a storm which hit in October of 1935, and repaired at a cost of $900, after which the club took on storm insurance. Then ten cabanas on the eastern end of the Beach were lost during the devastating "surprise" Hurricane of 1938. They were not rebuilt as the club had a surplus of available cabanas at the time. Another hurricane, in

The pool, from *Life Magazine* in 1946

Topless Sunbathing Prohibited

On May 12, 1937, the Executive Committee turned down a member's request to permit topless men's bathing suits at the Beach.

The deck at the Beach

No Smugglers, Please

In 1935 members were asked to use club liquor at the pool, rather than smuggle their own into cabanas.

November of 1950, destroyed the pier and tossed the cabanas east of the pool some thirty feet. At least twenty cabanas were a total loss, and they were replaced at a cost of $1,250 each, most of which was covered by insurance.

The cabanas originally were member owned, but have reverted back to the club upon their owners' death or resignation. Only one of the cabanas is still in the possession of a private owner, that being Lester Brion's on the far east end which is, with a wrap-around porch, the fanciest of the cabanas.

Water erosion has been an expensive and ongoing problem at the Beach. The bridge connecting the parking lot with the Beach, the only link between the Beach and the mainland, has been a problem for every Board from the very start, as has the dyke near the 14th tee, which controls the flow of water to and from the Sound.

There have been changes at the Beach, of

course. Policy changes, for example, like the relaxing of an old policy that forbade children in the pool between noon and 2 p.m. so that the adults might have a peaceful time for lunch—or a swim of their own.

Perhaps the first major physical change was the replacement circa 1940 of the aging boardwalk with concrete for safety reasons. The next changes came in the early 1960s when the pavilion underwent extensive rehabilitation, including a sprinkler system and an expanded and modernized kitchen. The club had acquired (in 1959) six acres west of the pavilion on which the children's play area was built, with space left over for additional parking. The wading pool was rebuilt at this time.

Next came the conversion from salt water to fresh water in the pool, which took place in 1965, mandated by the Board of Health. From the club's perspective, the change was necessary because the salt corroded the pool's piping, even though the water was changed three times a week. The pool had no filtration system then, and the water was not treated with chemicals. At first, the salt water was pumped in from the creek, later from the Sound, and the wading pool was filled from the main pool.

In 1967 ten new cabanas were built west of the casino, and the wading pool was eliminated, replaced by a relocated snack bar. The core of the building still consisted of two rooms, the main lounge and the smaller lounge closer to the Sound, which was totally enclosed by windows. The final four of the seventy-two cabanas, set well back from the Beach on the west side, were converted in the early 1970s from eight bath houses formerly used by Guthrie estate staff. Member Robert McKeon donated their conversion to the club in exchange for personal use of two of the cabanas.

During the years 1975 to 1978, during the presidency of Alfred J. Seaman, the casino's kitchen was expanded, and the kiddie area was supplemented with a jungle gym and roofed-over eating area. Also a 1,200-square-foot wooden deck, built on deep

View of the Sound from the East Casino

Harvey Gibson's Yacht Basin

Harvey Gibson's yacht basin was located just beyond the tenth green. He sailed to his Manhattan office each day on his yacht, called the *"Whisper,"* and when he returned at night, a small army of laborers was required to pull the vessel into its slip.

When Gibson set sail for Manhattan each morning, his chauffeur followed on land, heading for the city to meet the boat at the dock and transport Gibson to his office!

Cal with friends

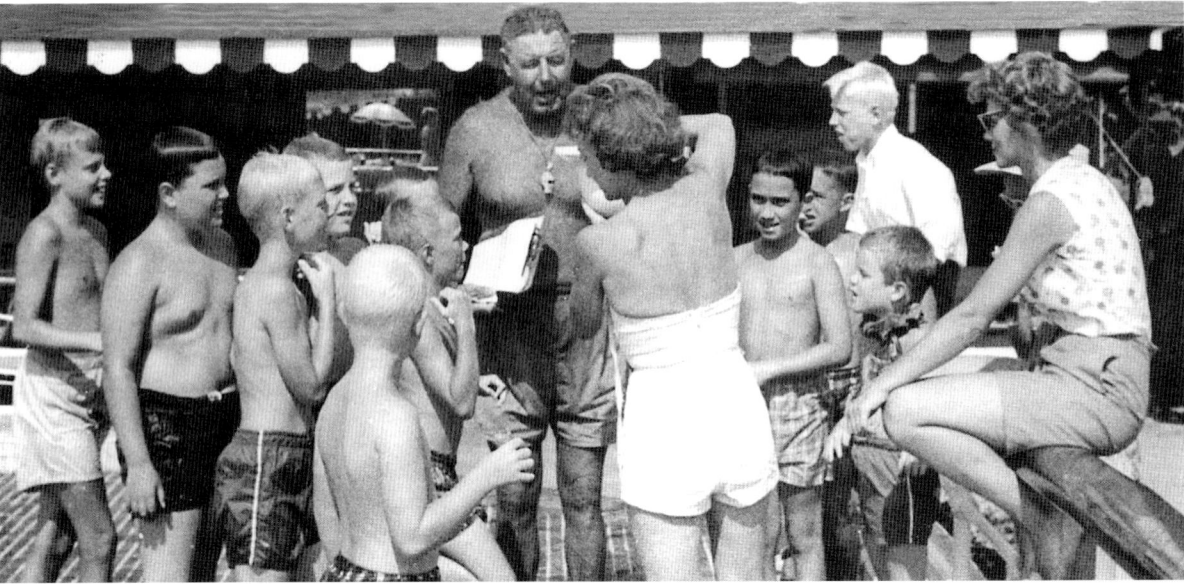

Cal & Ray

No discussion of the Beach would be complete without mention of certain individuals who have "made it work" over the years. John "Cal" Callahan was and still is a legendary figure as the swimming coach from 1938 through his retirement in 1969. Following brief tours by Dick Krempecki and Tom Liotti, Ray D'Annolfo and his veteran team of Jeff Converse and Angelo Stanco have followed in Cal's sandal-steps for the last twenty-two years. They helped make the Beach an informal, safe, child-friendly environment in which to learn to swim, compete, and just have a wonderful time. Indeed, the award for the outstanding swimmer each season is called the "Cal Award."

Angelo, Ray, and Jeff

On the watch

"Cal" played a major role in teaching the children of members how to swim, dive, and compete, not only among themselves but with other clubs on Long Island. In fact, Cal's relationship with many members actually preceded his Creek years, since he spent winters at the Bath & Tennis Club in Palm Beach, where many members' families spent their winters. It was not unusual for Cal to have taught the parents, and even grandparents, of the children he taught at The Creek in later years. And Cal did not just teach swimming. This very enthusiastic, adored man also ran birthday parties at the Beach for members' children; supervised the "traditional" Sunday races; and conducted swimming races between Piping Rock and The Creek.

Today, Ray D'Annolfo and his two long-standing assistants continue in the same tradition. Since coming to The Creek, Ray, together with his team, has brought The Creek swimming team into a more active inter-club league and swimming competitions, which has encouraged Creek swimmers to work hard to perfect their talents. Another successful activity, introduced by Cal and continued by Ray and his colleagues, is the swimming component of the Sports Group. For the record, Ray is still the "junior member" of the coaching staff, since Jeff and Angelo both started at The Creek in 1967 and have been invaluable members of The Creek Beach staff ever since.

The wading pool

> "Naturally a bathhouse on the beach, which is quite near Fox's Point, will help the heated golfer to enjoy the clear water of the Sound. Also a pier goes out to welcome the incoming yacht, so that the traveler by water can step off his boat on to the tenth tee and play the eighteen holes back to the ninth and go on his way rejoicing to the National or to New York. The organizing committee have thought of everything. And, after all, they have experience in this kind of thing. It hardly seems necessary to say that before the first of July, they will partake of the now well-known *character* of the Macdonald course, which means that both the golf and the food will be of the best."
>
> Town & Country
> February 1, 1923

pilings, was added, providing an outstanding place for beach-front dining, doubling the facility's dining area. The $23,000 deck project, completed in 1978, was financed by the sale of an original charcoal painting and seven George Bellows prints previously displayed in the Dormie House, netting $34,000.

In 1990 Nassau County investigators found that its health standards were not being met at the Beach, and threatened to shut the facility down. The County pointed out that the ship's railing around the pool was unsafe, the filtration system inadequate, the gutter system was overflowing improperly, and chemicals were emptying into the creek.

The club responded by spending in excess of $500,000 for renovations that included a new filtration and chlorination system and a new Cape Cod style gray picket fence was installed, surrounding an expanded deck for sunbathing. The weathered look of the fence blends nicely with its rustic environment.

The facility today features open-air dining on the deck and "under the roof" at the east end (a feature of the facility almost from the beginning), as well as a modern kitchen and indoor dining at

54 The Creek

Indoor dining at the Beach

the bar/lounge, plus an outside snack bar and eating area for the children. The cabanas extend from west of the casino, wrap around behind the building, passing east of the pool back to the Beach, then extend out even further along the Beach to the east, along the tenth fairway.

One tradition at the pool worth mentioning here are the Sunday afternoon races for the children, who compete in various age groups. There also are parent/children races. These races are an integral part of the "Swimming Awards Night" at the pool in late August, one of the social highlights of the season.

The Sailing and Beach Committe

In 1948 the club appointed a Sailing and Beach Committee to look into establishing a comprehensive sailing program and rehabilitating the Beach facilities. The following year, the committee suggested exchanging the club's aging boats for a new fleet that would provide for better sport, teaching the children the fine points of sailing. Unfortunately, the inlet has never been very conducive to sailing because of its lack of winds.

The Pine Room, as seen in 1933 when used as the living room

CHAPTER 8

Sailing Through Rough Waters

It is fair to say that our club had a troubled youth. The Creek's first quarter-century was punctuated by the Great Depression and World War II. Club life was disrupted by continuing problems with the lower holes of the golf course, and complicated by a merger with a neighboring club.

The first crisis faced by the new club was precipitated by George F. Baker, Jr. In the spring of 1926 Baker suddenly and unilaterally decided to extend the fence on the border of his property east of the club, in both directions, the northern extension reaching down to near the 18th tee, thereby cutting off both the service road and the road to the Beach. The club's engineers studied the situation, and eventually recommended building a new road to the Beach on the club's western boundary. The Board's initial reaction was that the club's finances prohibited such an expense, but the present road to the Beach was built, a $27,000 gift to the club by Clarence Mackay, as was a redirected service road costing $12,000, a gift from J. P. Morgan.

The club gained a measure of retribution when Baker requested, through his architects, that he be allowed to tap into the club's gas line for the house he was building for his daughter, and the club refused him.

The recurrent flooding of the lower holes was a problem almost from the start. The rise and fall of the tides, estimated at eight feet, flooded greens and left salt deposits on the fairways, preventing the grass from growing properly.

In the fall of 1926 the Green Committee recommended that these holes, especially the 12th, 13th, and 14th, not be "given up" because they were the best on the course. Green chairman Charles Blair Macdonald wanted to have the matter left in his hands, with an undetermined amount of money for the work needed to save the holes.

Macdonald suggested that the work would cost $20,000 to $30,000, but Board member Herbert Dean disagreed, stating that the holes required a complete reconstruction. He pointed out that he had asked the club's engineers to look at the situa-

Two views of the Garvan Room

tion closely, and that they suggested removing the top soil, putting in gravel and loam, then new top soil and new grass. Dean estimated the cost at $50,000, to be financed by an increase in membership if the funding could not be found in some other way. A bitter pill, he admitted, but necessary to prevent The Creek from becoming a 12-hole golf course.

Macdonald begrudgingly admitted that his engineers had made mistakes, and resigned from the club that winter. He was, however, quickly made The Creek's first honorary member. Herbert Dean became the new Green chairman.

Macdonald resigned as president of Kellenworth in 1931, and was succeeded in that capacity by Frank Crocker. Macdonald died in 1939.

Meanwhile, the Board began considering alternatives to rebuilding the lower holes. Part of the Gibson property was considered, but rejected, and in October of 1926, the Board decided to go ahead with "fixing" the lower holes at a cost of $50,000, raising the membership to 250 to finance the project. (The possibility of purchasing a portion of the Gibson property was an ongoing consideration for a number of years, a seemingly logical move the Board never felt could be financed.)

But when the estimated cost of reconstruction grew to $75,000, the Board considered instead property owned by George Baker and Tom Lamont (a J. P. Morgan partner) on the club's eastern flank, on which no more than two new holes could be built, and asked Dean to investigate more closely. Apparently, the Board preferred the idea of adding to the club's assets rather than improving existing assets.

By the start of the 1927 golfing season, no decision had been made on the fate of the lower holes. By then there was no chance of buying additional land, and the reconstruction job would take eighteen months to complete, another deterrent in addition to the cost.

Nonetheless, at its July 20 meeting, the Board recommended spending the necessary funds to repair these holes, to be paid by some combination of assessment, increasing the mortgage, or member gifts. The plan was approved, although the option of financing by assessment was deleted. At the end of the year, Dean reported that it would be necessary to raise the entire area of the lower holes several feet, and that the work would start the following March. The project would involve dredging, and the delivery and spreading of up to 8,000 cubic yards of loam and top soil. In addition, the tidal gates had been condemned, and had to be rebuilt at an additional cost of $10,400.

The membership loaned the club $55,000 of the needed funding, and Kellenworth provided the last $20,000. It was hoped that the holes would be playable by late 1928 or the spring of 1929 at the latest. Harvey Gibson suggested that financial aid was available at New York Trust at a slightly higher rate over a longer period than the existing mortgage.

The problems did not end there. An April 1929 storm caused a breach in the dyke, putting the newly-revised golf course in grave danger. The club's engineer recommended a new dyke, raised above the old one, at a cost of almost $30,000. This proved to be money well spent. The fall tides of 1929 were the highest in thirty years, the water level rising to within one foot of the top of the new dyke.

The Beach area had more storms to face in the coming decade. A storm in the fall of 1932 caused beach erosion near the tenth green. The Hurricane of 1938 damaged four of the water holes, creating again the need for some reconstruction, which cost $6,400 including reseeding. The lower holes were out of play until July of 1939. Other clubs fared far worse; Maidstone lost its golf courses for more than a year following this vicious storm. Finally, the Hurricane of 1950 broke the flood gate at the 14th tee and flooded five holes.

Alexander Richie was appointed green keeper and groundskeeper in 1928, and by 1934 the course was considered to be in its best condition ever. By that time, most of the greens had been remodeled, with an eye toward providing proper drainage.

In December of 1934, the Board acted to provide ongoing oversight, rewriting the club's Rules to limit the power of the Green Committee so that the committee could make no material change to the golf course without the permission of the Board.

Regarding the club's governance, the Board discussed the need to appoint an Executive Committee to oversee club operations more closely, meet more regularly, and afford committee chairmen the opportunity to report more reg-

The Dormie House as seen in 1932

ABOVE: The tennis hut as seen from the courts
BELOW: A member's plane taxis into the Beach

ularly. The committee was created in May 1926, and met for the first time in June.

In 1929 the Green Committee appointed the new five-man Golf Committee. The club also organized an Aviation Committee in 1937, its purpose to regulate, for safety reasons, members flying to and landing their seaplanes at the club.

The club quickly faced the need for additional clubhouse facilities, and the sum of $100,000 for additions and extensions to the building was approved at the December 1927 Board meeting. Plans drawn up by architect James Gamble Rogers were presented in January and approved.

The expanded clubhouse reopened on July 2, 1928, with relatively symmetric wings added to both the east and west ends of the building. The formal Dining Room was built by expanding the butler's pantry southward, then adding what is now the breakfast room on the east end, originally as a staging area for the wait staff. This balanced two rooms imported to the club, and attached at the western end of the building. The Garvan (Card) Room, said to be a genuine McIntyre Room, was in its previous existence part of a home in Salem, Massachusetts, while the Pine Room is believed to have come either from a farmhouse near Philadelphia, or from a Manhattan apartment indirectly from New England, perhaps Salem. Both were gifts to the club from Francis P. Garvan, who had both rooms redecorated at his own expense.

The Pine Room, once referred to as the "fireside dining room," and now an informal dining room/pub, originally was a living room. The antique wood flooring is believed to be very old, and both the wood and paneling in that room are looked upon as one of the club's greatest assets. The painting over the fireplace appears to have been done directly on the paneling.

Later that year, the Board approved keeping the building open all winter rather than closing it after Thanksgiving, as had been the practice.

In 1935 the Tennis Committee suggested first that a tennis house be built, and later that two more courts were needed. The house was built in 1935, and the new Har Tru courts were approved in October, and opened the following May, located to the south of the existing courts. Their $5,500 cost was covered almost entirely by interested members.

The members also had the use of an indoor court nearby, on the estate of Harold I. Pratt off Dosoris Road in Glen Cove, ten minutes from the club. That court was leased, for an annual fee of $1,000, including maintenance.

And then in 1940 the Tennis Committee expressed their desire for additional land on which grass courts could be built. This request was tabled for almost a decade.

The Depression and ensuing war years proved fatal to many American golf and country clubs, financial exigencies forcing them to close their doors forever. The Creek did not escape unscathed, but survived in relatively good fashion. Membership dropped to 215 after the 1932 season, when the Depression reached its depths. Wages of employees were cut 10 percent that year, a move which caused the resignation of the entire House Committee in protest. The club operated at a profit during 1933 by cutting costs for meals, golf, and swimming by 30 to 40 percent, "the times being what they are." That would be the last year for a while during which the club would operate "in the black."

The club faced a serious deficit in 1934, when membership dropped below 200, spending $25,000 more than collected from dues ($350). The Board identified four options to balance the club's budget: new members, increased club usage, further economies, or outings.

And so, in April of 1935 the original policy of having just one class of membership was altered. At that time, three classes were established, with most of the existing members falling into the class called "Founders," implying they owned shares of Kellenworth stock. New members joining in this class had to buy stock and pay a $1,000 initiation fee.

The new classifications, designed to attract prospective young members, were called "Associate" (no stock, same initiation fee and assessments, and no voting or proprietary rights) and "Junior," which was restricted to applicants aged eighteen to twenty-nine, with no stock or initiation fee, and no vote. Associate and Junior members were made eligible to serve on the Board in 1936. To help the younger members, the Green Committee recommended in 1939 that green fees and other charges be lowered.

To help retain members in financial difficulty, Kellenworth offered to buy their shares in lieu of dues. Members forced to resign during the Depression were allowed to return to membership without an initiation fee and much of the red tape usually accompanying application for membership.

By mid 1939, membership had climbed back to 260. In 1940 a classification called "Annual Subscribers" was established for widows, upon invitation.

The tennis courts

BELOW: Overview of the first two tennis courts and fifth green in the late 1920s

Women's National founders (left to right): Mrs. W. A. Gavin, Alexa Stirling, Marion Hollins, Mrs. Quentin Feitner (Lillian Hyde), and Mrs. G. M. Heckscher

CHAPTER 9

Women's National

At about the time The Creek came into existence, there also was born the Women's National Golf & Tennis Club nearby in Glen Head. Exclusively for women, some felt its creation was a reaction to the presence of the all-male Links Club a few miles away in Searingtown, others to overcrowded conditions at nearby clubs (such as Piping Rock and Nassau) that left women with little opportunity to play golf on weekends.

Women's National opened on Memorial Day of 1924, fulfilling the dream of Marion Hollins, the daughter of H. B. Hollins, first president of the Metropolitan Golf Association. Marion Hollins was an outstanding all-around athlete and equestrian, and quite possibly the most influential woman of golf's first half-century in America. An accomplished player, she won the United States Women's Amateur at Hollywood (New Jersey) in 1921, and the Women's Metropolitan championship three times (1913, 1919, and 1924). The idea of an exclusive women's club was in the back of her mind for several years, and after winning the "National" in 1921, she channeled her energies toward making it a reality. A 160-acre site in Glen Head was acquired early in 1922, and work began soon thereafter. Devereux Emmet was contracted to design and build the golf course, and both Charles Blair Macdonald and Seth Raynor consented to help with suggestions.

Taking a leaf from Macdonald's book, Hollins visited England in the spring of 1922, and studied a score of courses there, taking detailed notes on holes or specific features of holes she particularly liked. These were then presented to Emmet upon her return. Consequently, the Women's National, like Macdonald's National Golf Links, included several holes that were virtual copies of British holes, and others that embodied superlative features found on British courses. Aside from an

Marion Hollins

adaptation of the Principal's Nose at St. Andrews, however, Hollins' copies came from courses such as Walton Heath, Northampton, and Mid-Surrey near London, the fifth at Macdonald's National, the 13th at his Piping Rock, and the fifth at her father's Westbrook at East Islip.

Emmet's mandate was to design a course that wouldn't defeat the better women players with excessive length, yet continually challenge with the clever placement of its hazards. At most tees the player faced a challenging carry, although an alternate route was always provided, typically at the loss of one stroke, for those unwilling or unable to challenge the hazard. The placement of these hazards was keyed to the average carry of one of three-time national champion Alexa Stirling's drives, which was estimated to be 175 yards. Although the greens too were well trapped, there were entrances, and run-up shots were usually possible, provided the drive was reasonably placed. The putting surfaces were relatively level, with only a few of them possessing severe undulations. When the club opened, the course played to a par of 74 at 5,879 yards.

An old-fashioned Colonial farmhouse on the property was moved to a high knoll overlooking the golf course in all directions, and converted into a clubhouse. Two wings were added to accommodate locker space and a dining room. In addition, club facilities featured twenty-two tennis courts, including eleven of the finest grass courts in the world, and stables to accommodate those members active with the local hunt set.

The membership goal at Women's National was 400, which was attained prior to the opening, and surpassed prior to the Depression. Most of the members hailed from the Metropolitan area, including a good number whose husbands belonged to The Creek and Piping Rock, but the membership roster did span the nation. Among the members were Edith Cummings, the national amateur champion of 1923, and Lillian Hyde (Mrs. Quentin Feitner), a four-time champion of the WMGA. Rosalie Knapp, later to become Mrs. Joseph Dey, Jr., served as president of the WMGA during the years 1935 to 1937 while a member at Women's National, as was her mother.

Ernest Jones, recognized as one of the great golf teachers in the world despite the handicap of having lost a leg while serving in the British army during World War I, held sway as professional at Women's National, and developed an excellent reputation as a teacher of ladies.

Once Women's National had been launched, and she had served her term as the club's first president, Marion Hollins spent a good amount of time on the West Coast, on the Monterrey Peninsula in particular. Cypress Point was another of her creations, as was the Pasatiempo Country Club in Santa Cruz, at the northern end of Monterrey Bay. Marion Hollins died in 1944 after being seriously injured in an automobile accident, and apparently had very little, if anything, to do with the merger of the club she founded with The Creek.

ABOVE: Alexa Stirling
BELOW: The athletic Marion Hollins in action on the polo field

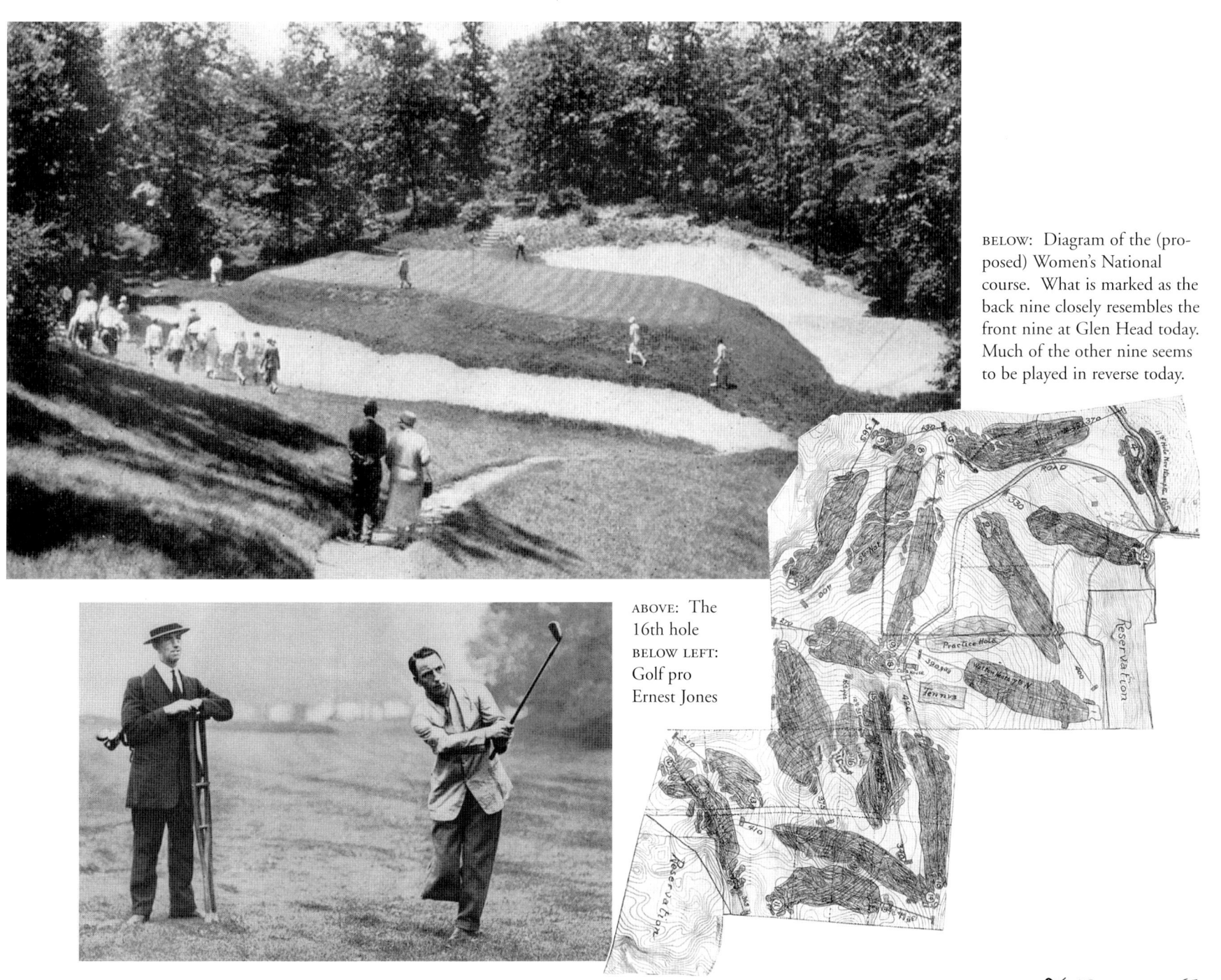

BELOW: Diagram of the (proposed) Women's National course. What is marked as the back nine closely resembles the front nine at Glen Head today. Much of the other nine seems to be played in reverse today.

ABOVE: The 16th hole
BELOW LEFT: Golf pro Ernest Jones

The Creek 65

The bowling alleys, center of one of the club's
most popular social activities during the 1940s

CHAPTER 10

The Cedar Creek Club

No sooner had this country emerged from the depths of the Depression when the outbreak of war in Europe precluded any thought of a return to the lifestyle of the twenties. During the years just prior to the United States' entry into World War II, a number of golf and country clubs found themselves operating at a deficit, and their very existence in jeopardy. The Creek and Piping Rock were no exceptions, although in nowhere near as dire straits as Women's National. Although that club's membership count reached as high as 450 by 1931, Women's National, because of its specialized nature, had difficulty raising money and suffered through the Depression.

At a meeting of the Creek's Board on April 2, 1941, with no president in place following the death of Clarence Mackay two years earlier, a possible merger with Piping Rock was discussed, but by month's end, the disadvantages of such a move—crowded conditions at the Beach and on the golf course, and the closing down of one of two outstanding facilities—became apparent, and the issue was dropped.

Instead, on April 27, a merger with Women's National was suggested. A committee of five was quickly appointed to discuss the possibility with Women's National. On that committee were Harvey Gibson, the club's newly elected president, Paul G. Pennoyer, Henry P. Davison, Jr., Edward L. Shea, and Dudley H. Mills. The Women's Consolidation Committee consisted of Mrs. Joseph E. Davis, Mrs. Harold I. Pratt, and Mrs. J. Cornelius Rathborne.

Very little time was wasted. By May 8, a formal plan for merger was proposed to the Boards of both clubs, and accepted. Formed as a result was the Cedar Creek Club, with both facilities remaining open and fully operational. The two golf courses were called the "Creek Course" and the "Cedar Course," and the clubhouses were known as the "Creek House" and the "Cedar House." At the time, Women's had 270 members, including 43 whose husbands belonged to The Creek, and The Creek had 240 members. What made the merger work were the economies in operation

The Cedar Creek logo

The Skeet House

Skeet Shooting at The Creek

Skeet originally had been proposed by member George Gale in 1935, but the Board thought that the noise from a field on the adjacent Lamont property would upset the club's neighbors. Consequently, skeet was tabled, only to be reintroduced in 1941, with the field to be placed on the Cedar grounds since the Board still believed it unlikely The Creek's neighbors would approve. Ultimately, neighborhood restrictions prevented the start of shooting before 9:30 a.m.

It was not until the end of the winter of 1947-1948, however, that the club's skeet facility was (partially) opened. The field was located east of the 18th fairway, and a small clapboard building on the grounds was moved there as headquarters for the club's shooters, who numbered approximately twenty. Eventually, the members competed in a three-club league with Piping Rock and Rockaway Hunting Club. In 1961 a land swap with the school district for the Locust Valley High School gave the club room to develop a quail walk and redirect the shooting away from the school property.

It was the sale of the Gibson property alongside the 14th hole in 1979, and its subsequent development into home sites, that led to the demise of skeet at The Creek in October of 1989. The possibility of a stray shot landing on a neighbor's property, as well as the noise factor, were concerns too significant to ignore any longer. And so the club's skeet group now shoots elsewhere, as guests of neighboring clubs.

---

effected. The "joint operation of departments" meant one golf professional, one tennis professional, one general manager, and one green superintendent, each overseeing two facilities. In the winter months (mid-November through mid-May), plans were to close the Cedar Course and the Creek House, while continuing to operate the Dormie House and Cedar House.

The members of Women's National were protected against The Creek's much larger mortgage ($340,000 compared with $19,000) in the consolidation. From their perspective, the primary advantages of the merger were the Beach and an additional interesting golf course. Their restaurant service was shut down, but wasn't being utilized very much at the time anyway. For Creek members, there was an additional golf course, grass tennis courts, overnight facilities at the Cedar House, and a reduction in dues to $250.

What resulted was a unique club, with two very different golf courses, all kinds of tennis courts, and a beach. The initiation fee was set at $200. Most important, the merger gave both clubs a new lease on life.

The Certificate of Consolidation was dated May 23. The new club was to have just "regular" members, consolidating all three membership classes at The Creek and two at Women's National. There would also be Life and Honorary members. The membership count was a healthy 522. The new club adopted the Creek bird as the focus of its logo.

The first meeting of the Cedar Creek Club took place on June 15, with Harvey Gibson, who had been elected the merged club's first president, as chairman and Paul Pennoyer as secretary. The business of the day was surprising: the proposal of a new skeet range, and the suggestion that the club add bowling as a feature, following the lead of the Wee Burn Club in Darien, Connecticut.

The go-ahead for installing four bowling lanes at the Creek House (rather than at the Cedar House, as originally proposed) was given on July 22. A wing was quickly added to the western end of the clubhouse, and "opening night" was held on Monday evening, November 3. The financing ($12,000) came on loan from interested members, who were repaid by 1947. By then bowling had become so popular at The Creek (dinner and bowling on Wednesday and Thursday nights) that the annual bowling dinner-dance became one of the club's leading social functions. Interclub bowling matches with Piping Rock had been ongoing since 1942. Automatic pinsetters were installed in 1960.

Perhaps the dominant figure in Creek bowling over the years has been Mrs. George C. Meyer, eighteen times the ladies' champion, and author of the highest game ever by a Creek woman, 229. Earl Ellis bowled the highest game in club history, a 274 in 1992.

By the fall of 1941 the specter of the large mortgage on the Creek property cast a long shadow over Board meetings. That financial obligation was far too heavy considering the club's dues schedule. The governors considered several options: (a) to renegotiate the mortgage with New York Trust; (b) to sell the Creek property and relocate entirely at Cedar; (c) to sell Creek, and merge Cedar with Meadow Brook (then located on the outskirts of Garden City, between Roosevelt Field and Hempstead Turnpike); or (d) to renegotiate the lease arrangement with Kellenworth. Ultimately, the decision was made to renegotiate the mortgage with New York Trust on more favorable terms: a lower rate over a longer period of time.

Nonetheless, the club seemed very upbeat, accepting an offer in November 1941 to use the pond on the Lamont property for winter skating. Mrs. Whitney Bourne donated a portable cabin for the skaters, but by 1946, the club decided to abandon the pond for lack of interest.

The Cedar House opened for the 1942 season on May 1, with long-term room rentals assigned there and transients to the Creek House. Both golf courses were in the best of shape, and

The Cedar House lounge

Dorothy Randle was the new tennis professional at the Cedar courts.

However, with the country at war and a growing number of members in the service (with 75 percent of their dues remitted), revenue was greatly curtailed and it became obvious from a financial standpoint that it was going to be difficult to keep even one course open.

As early as February of 1943, club activities were at a virtual standstill due to wartime restrictions. A War Emergency Committee was formed to act, at its own discretion, under national wartime restrictions, on any and all matters relating to the operation of the club.

It was as much for the spirit of the membership as anything else that the club decided to operate at both locations, with nine holes at Cedar and nine holes at Creek, dirt (no grass) courts open at Cedar, the Beach and Dormie House open, but the Creek clubhouse closed (except the bowling alleys), and the Cedar House and overnight rooms open.

The Red Cross was offered work space in both clubhouses, and facilities were offered for life saving courses, home nursing, and community caring. During the war years, military personnel were offered the use of the golf course, enlisted men free of charge during the week, officers on weekends for $1. Wounded servicemen from Mitchell Field were entertained for bowling and lunch one day each week, and every other Wednesday at the Beach. This program was subsidized by member contributions.

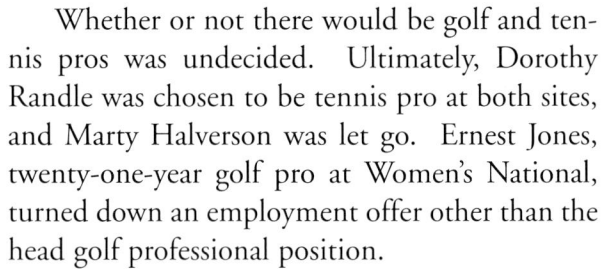

Whether or not there would be golf and tennis pros was undecided. Ultimately, Dorothy Randle was chosen to be tennis pro at both sites, and Marty Halverson was let go. Ernest Jones, twenty-one-year golf pro at Women's National, turned down an employment offer other than the head golf professional position.

When the Links Club course in Searingtown (a club created by C. B. Macdonald) was closed for the duration, its members were offered use of the Cedar Creek facilities. So, too, were Piping Rock members. In a similar vein, Deepdale extended the courtesies of its club and course to our members.

By April 6, however, plans had changed. Because of the manpower situation, gasoline rationing, and other wartime curtailments affecting civilian life, the club decided to center all activities at The Creek and close Cedar for the season. With many of the members between twenty-one and fifty years of age called from their homes in the community for the duration of the war, the demand for a full 36-hole facility did not exist. At The Creek, the remaining members enjoyed tennis, 18 holes of golf, the Beach, and bowling. The golf course and grass courts at Cedar were to be preserved for future use by cutting only, but the grass died by mid July 1944. Restoration was put on hold, then later completely dismissed.

One primary consideration in this decision was the club's children, and the need to give them a common meeting ground. Dorothy Randle came to Creek from Cedar that summer to give tennis lessons, and instituted a junior tennis pro-

The Cedar House patio

gram, which was run successfully by Lillian Hester and Martha Crisp through Randle's retirement in 1951. There were organized play classes for the children as well. The club also inaugurated a summer Beach membership, costing $50, limited to fifty people in the community who were not members of the club. To further economize, the club canceled its lease on the indoor tennis court at the Pratt estate in Glen Cove in May of 1945, following Pratt's death earlier in the year. The club also refurbished several single rooms in the Dormie House for bachelor members unable to travel to and from the club.

The membership roster dwindled steadily during the war years, a number of defections being former Women's National members who were miffed that their club had been abandoned. The head count went as low as 396 by mid-May of 1944, with 86 of these in the service. Nonetheless, there was great activity on the Creek golf course.

There was a minor fire in the clubhouse on May 12, 1944, which was extinguished quickly by employees and the Locust Valley fire department. The living room, west wing rest rooms, and roof suffered mostly water damage, fully covered by insurance. The living room had to be closed temporarily for repairs, otherwise the members suffered little inconvenience. As part of the repair process, the club installed two more guest rooms on the second floor.

By the fall of 1944, with Mrs. Winthrop W. Aldrich acting chair (she was actually the first vice president, acting as president in the absence of Harvey Gibson, who was in Europe with the Red Cross; her husband was later named the United States Ambassador to the United Kingdom), the Board voted to offer the Cedar property for lease at an annual rate of $2,500, the fixed charges on the Cedar property, which was generating no revenue at the time. David Cowles, representing the Penguin Club in Manhattan, made an offer to lease the Cedar House for three years at that rate, also intimating that he would spend $8,000 to put the house in first-class condition. His intent was to operate an upscale restaurant in the house. An agreement with the Penguin Club was signed on October 26, 1944, the three-year lease to commence on February 1, 1945.

By 1945 the Board of Governors included two husband-and-wife tandems, Mr. and Mrs. Harvey Gibson and Mr. and Mrs. Dudley H. Mills, and the club's (combined) membership was 407. With war's end, a Management Board was established to survey the club's operations and assess the needs of the various constituencies.

By mid-season, the club had been approached about selling the Cedar property, and in October received an offer of $150,000 for the facility from Benjamin Ribman, representing the Fresh Meadow Country Club. Fresh Meadow at the time was located in Queens, just south of the

The Cedar House library

> *Anybody for . . . TV?*
>
> On September 24, 1947, a group of members presented to the club a rather new and revolutionary gift: a Philco television set. This quickly resulted in a popular new adjunct to club life: television picnics. For the small sum of $1.50, a member was entitled to a small supper and the privilege of watching the television.

present-day Long Island Expressway, surrounded by advancing civilization. The Creek's reaction at the time was to hold on to the property in anticipation of a postwar rise in land values. Within the year, Fresh Meadow purchased its present site from the failing Lakeville Club.

It was not until September 19, 1946, that the Board softened its previous position that the Cedar property was not for sale. It now declared that any offer would be taken under consideration, and that the property might be sold, but not for less than $250,000, with $100,000 in cash.

By 1947 the Penguin Club had allowed the Cedar property to run down badly. The plumbing was leaking, the paint was peeling, and dogs were living in the house—deplorable conditions, indeed. In addition, rent payments were long past due.

By May, the club had decided to sell the property, and was entertaining three offers, one from a group representing the United Nations, a second from the Sound View Country Club, which had just sold its property in Great Neck, and the third from a man who operated a public course (possibly Engineers, which was public at the time) and wanted another. A prospective deal with the United Nations group was the first to fall through. After pondering the possibility of allowing general manager Jacob Kramer and green superintendent Jock Dishington to operate the course as a public facility for the club's profit, the Board finally decided that the Sound View group offered the better deal.

And so on July 7, 1947, the Board arranged with the Glen Head Holding Corporation, a group of former members of Sound View who earlier in the year had unsuccessfully attempted to purchase the Engineers course, to lease the facilities for three years, starting February 15, 1948, at an annual rental of $20,000, plus taxes. It was understood that Glen Head would spend up to $50,000 to improve conditions over the first eighteen months, and the new club was given an option to purchase for $300,000 in 1951. This agreement with the newly formed Glen Head Country Club was consummated on October 17, 1947, and Glen Head did, in fact, exercise its option to purchase in 1951. The golf course, which had not been used for several years, was rejuvenated, and some eighty traps were eliminated to make it more enjoyable for the average club player.

In 1946 the Cedar Creek Club faced and ultimately resolved another problem of long standing. The mortgage which had been placed on The Creek to meet the overrun in cost when the club was built called for certain amortizations each year, but as these were not insisted upon by the holder of the mortgage, only a few of these payments had been made. In fact during the first twenty years of the existence of the club, the mortgage had been amortized only to the extent of $45,000, and when World War II ended, the amount still outstanding was $308,000. This placed a heavy burden on the club's operating budget, amounting to $20,400 per annum. The mortgage had been in default several times, but because of the State Mortgage Moratorium regulations, and by virtue of various special agreements made, the operation of the club was not greatly impacted. The mortgage, however, came due on April 1, 1947.

Throughout 1946 and into 1947, negotiations were carried on with the New York Trust Company in an endeavor to obtain from them some relief in the shape of an offer on their part to sell the mortgage to the club at a discount in the event that some plan could be worked out to finance such a transaction. These negotiations, although seeming fairly favorable at first, failed due to the greatly increased values of desirable suburban properties such as that of Cedar Creek. The New York Trust Company terminated all negotiations by giving a final answer that they were convinced that the property could be disposed of in case of foreclosure of the mortgage at maturity at its full face value, hence would not consider selling the mortgage at any discount whatsoever.

It was obvious, therefore, that some arrangements had to be made by the club to meet the situation on or before April 1. With that end in view, negotiations were initiated with other interests, with the result that a tentative plan was worked out that seemed highly advantageous to the Cedar Creek Club, affording the club the first reasonable opportunity in its history to refinance its mortgage indebtedness and thereby greatly improve its financial situation. In essence, the club retired the Kellenworth mortgage by taking a $190,000 loan from an educational foundation and selling $118,000 worth of certificates to Creek members. Two trust funds were established to amortize these two loans. And finally, in 1963 the Kellenworth Corporation was dissolved after The Creek took title to the property.

Harvey Gibson, who was the club's president throughout these difficult years (from 1941 until his death in 1950) had the following perspective on the ultimate resolution of the club's financial problems.

"We had hardly completed formulation of our plans for postwar operations when, like a bolt out of the blue, the holder of the mortgage demanded payment in full. Although meeting the demand presented a most difficult problem, we immediately worked out a financial reorganization of the club which was carried through successfully. As I look back on it, I am glad that the demand for payment was made because it forced upon us our successful financial reorganization which put us in splendid shape. Not long after, the Women's National premises were sold to another golf club which further strengthened the financial position of the merged club."

By October, following the resolution of the Kellenworth mortgage, dues were set at $250 for the club's 451 members. The club planned to reduce the membership to 400 by admitting one new member for each two that retired or passed away.

And finally, on July 1, 1948, the club changed its name back to the one with which it was founded: The Creek, Inc.

The indoor tennis court at the Pratt estate. Photograph by Monica Randall

Tennis at The Creek

CHAPTER II

The Racquets Renaissance

By the advent of the 1950s, The Creek had assumed its original name—and its original personality. The club was staid, very formal. Golf was king. For the next two decades, members of the Beach and Tennis Committees were continually reminded, "This is a golf club," whenever they asked for funding for improvements or expansion in their own domains of interest.

In the early 1950s, The Creek was not especially "children-friendly," and the Board did little to make the club attractive to (prospective) young families. Attempts at children's programs at the Beach sputtered. Consequently, even some legacy members looked elsewhere for a family club, and Piping Rock often was the beneficiary.

A program at the Beach, originally called the "Sports Group," was first attempted in the late forties by member William Ylvisaker and soon canceled because of too few children. It was introduced again in 1959 (and formally accepted as a club activity in 1963) by four of the club's women, Mrs. William Eakins, Mrs. James Finlayson, Mrs. A. J. Powers, and Mrs. Noel Ryan, as a summer diversion for their sons, and other boys of their age. The group welcomed girls the following year, and has since flourished. Most of its activities were beach-oriented, run by college-aged counselors, and overseen closely by the mothers.

Tennis was included in the Sports Group activities, as was baseball, on a field established at the foot of the driving range (where the club once contemplated an athletic "complex" for the children, something more elaborate than just a ball field). In the early years, the children walked from one activity to the next; today they are transported by bus. A golf component never materialized, perhaps because the children involved were too young.

"Great match!"

A group of girls in the Sports Group in 1967

Boys in the Sports Group in 1969

76   The Creek

The program was opened to Piping Rock children in 1973, when not filled by Creek children.

The club's four tennis courts, out beyond the fifth green, were supplemented in 1947 by an additional two courts to the south, and the six courts were very active in the early 1950s, so much so that both women and children were expected to step aside on weekends when the (working) men wished to play. But tennis suffered through a nation-wide downtrend during the 1950s into the 1960s, while golf, with Arnold Palmer, then Jack Nicklaus, carrying the banner, enjoyed a halcyon era.

In 1959 the Board proposed a five-year master plan that would affect all phases of club life. Included was the purchase of some five acres west of the pool for a play area and additional parking, as well as the rebuilding of the wading pool and a modern kitchen for the Beach pavilion; an extended irrigation system to bring water to the lower holes; an expansion of the golf shop together with new stairs to the roof, where a porch was to be built for golfers waiting at the first tee; two additional tennis courts, as well as having the old courts resurfaced and fenced in, the tennis shop enlarged, and the parking lot extended; and the construction of two platform tennis courts.

Also, four more cottages, for rental to members without children, either as a permanent home or as an alternative to their Manhattan apartments, located down the 18th hole below the White cottage, which appears to have been on the grounds from the very beginning of the club; acoustical ceilings for the Gibson Room and bowling alleys; automatic pinsetters and air-conditioning for the bowling alleys; and modernized heating and electrical systems for the main buildings.

Also contemplated at this time was a land trade that would provide a new location for the skeet field and driving range. The club anticipated (incorrectly) having the old site condemned in conjunction with the building of the new Locust Valley High School on land adjacent to club property. (The club did surrender twelve acres, not including the range.)

The master plan was approved, and implemented piecemeal over the next several years, its $200,000 price tag financed by assessments. The installation of pinsetters, construction of the cottages, and the pro shop expansion all took place in 1960. The Beach improvements were accomplished in the early 1960s during the presidency of John C. Wood.

Tennis made a comeback in the mid 1960s, but when the club's tennis advocates sought expansion, they had to contend, not just with the Board, but also with the club's neighbors and local zoning laws. Although the Board approved two new courts south of the existing setup, zoning laws prevented the construction of more than one new Har Tru court in 1967. The seventh court was squeezed in between the older middle courts and the fifth green, and was achieved after much opposition from the golfers, who felt the court would intrude upon the fifth hole. The old courts were resurfaced the following year, all paid for by the tennis players.

Preceding this tennis renaissance came the introduction of platform (or paddle) tennis in 1963. Board member Jim Keresey provided the inspiration, reviving an idea he first proposed in 1959, while Jimmy Minsky added the perspiration, to introduce the new activity to the club and nurture it through childhood into a thriving adjunct to club life. Platform tennis grew in popularity to the extent that at one time it was necessary to reserve a playing time on Thursday, Friday, and Saturday nights.

The club's paddle tennis facility, located between the first and second holes, consisted of two wooden courts which were ready for play in the fall of 1963. A warming hut came next, in 1967, followed by a third court in 1971, while the conversion to aluminum decks with heated surfaces and lighting all came later.

As paddle flourished, its Member-Guest Dinner Dance became the major winter function at the club. Interest in paddle fell off, however, after the opening of the indoor facility, and one court was lost in 1995. Nonetheless, the club fields three men's teams and one ladies' team, which play once or twice a week in league competition. The

ABOVE: One of the newer cottages
BELOW: The White cottage

ABOVE: The paddle courts
ABOVE RIGHT: The championship 1993–1994 paddle tennis team

men's "A" team is made up of Creek and Piping Rock players; this team won the 1993-1994 "A" Division championship of the Long Island Paddle Tennis Association.

Despite thriving racquets programs, an outstanding golf course, and the unique Beach, The Creek experienced difficulties in the early 1970s, when the oil crisis and decline on Wall Street complicated an already downward trend for the country's golf clubs. Indeed, there was talk once again of a possible merger with Piping Rock. The solution at The Creek was quite simple: youth, and even more emphasis on racquets.

In 1972 The Creek instituted a "summer membership" program that proved very fruitful, seeding the flow of new young members into the club. The program allowed potential full members the opportunity to use the facilities for one summer season, allowing them to become acquainted with the club, and vice-versa, thereby facilitating the admissions process.

Bill Douglas was the club's tennis pro throughout this period of decline and rejuvenation. He started in 1960, along with his wife Eileen, who ran the tennis shop which, then as now, was located near the fifth green.

In Douglas' next-to-last season (1972), the club hired David Bannard as assistant tennis professional. Bannard was the No. 1 player on the Princeton University tennis team. His dictate was to establish a junior program in tennis. In a short time, that program would flourish, and be incorporated into the Sports Group, whose scope would be widened to include tennis and golf as well as beach activities (swimming and sailing).

This new focus on tennis proved to be a significant turning point in club history, attracting prospective young men, with young families, to

50th Anniversary Celebration

The Creek celebrated its Golden Jubilee Weekend on September 28-29, 1973, the highlight of the festivities being a gala black tie dinner dance on Saturday evening. Lester Lanin and his band, longtime favorites of the membership (Lanin got his start at The Creek), performed for the occasion. The club operated full blast all weekend, with spirited competitions and sociable activities.

The weekend was blessed with absolutely gorgeous fall weather, The festivities actually began on Friday evening, with dinner followed by a bowling competition and bridge and backgammon games. Saturday featured round-robin tennis and paddle tournaments and best ball of foursome golf, at full handicaps, with each foursome composed of men and/or women as the members chose. Sunday's fare included croquet (on the south lawn in front of the clubhouse) starting at noon, and an epic softball game matching the over-forties against the under-forties. As the weekend's program noted, "All spectators over forty are subject to being drafted as players, as fatigue overcomes the starting team."

The festivities concluded at 5:00 p.m. with a cocktail party and awards ceremony, presided over by club president George F. Baker, Jr., with Ralph Smith as anniversary chairman and member and radio personality John A. Gambling as master of ceremonies.

---

apply for membership. Both parents, with demands on their time from work or children, found a relatively quick tennis match more realistic than a four-hour round of golf.

The construction of the first two "lower courts," located "down below," on the far side of the Dormie House, north of the Tower House, took place in 1972 during the presidency of George F. Baker, Jr. There was talk about whether the new courts would be indoors, under a "bubble," but when the membership was polled on the matter, there proved to be little support for the unsightly "bubble," a sentiment that was echoed by the club's neighbors. The original proposal for an indoor tennis facility included squash, but this part was voted down.

The new courts eventually were built outdoors, the first two Har Tru in 1972, and the final two in 1976, hard surface courts for all-season play and use with the sports group and junior tennis clinics that were started in 1972, on the heels of the construction of the first two new courts. The courts also attracted overflow member play, but the tennis afficionados preferred to play at the original site near their fifth hole.

A storm the night before the first two lower courts were to open nearly postponed opening day, which was saved when the members removed the sod washed onto the courts while the builder, James Finlayson (whose father's business, Finlayson & Hinkle, had built the Beach pavilion and cabanas), rebuilt the terraced hillside next to the courts.

The club's growing interest in tennis was accelerated with the appointment in 1974 of Harrison and Kit Knight as tennis professionals. Their mission was simple: they were told to develop a strong junior program. The results

The lower tennis courts

were far reaching: players of all skills and ages were able to enjoy tennis. In one case, they transformed an adult beginner into a club champion in less than ten years. In 1989 one of their top junior students, Joanna Shea, became the first Creek woman to win Piping Rock's Brady Cup, a prestigious nine-club grass court competition. She repeated her victory in 1990. The year 1989 also witnessed the emergence of the most dominant ladies' club champion in Creek history, with Mrs. Stuart "Mimi" Hartmeyer winning her first of nine championships in ten years. The Knight's program wasn't just for the elite players, either. They made the "B" and "C" players an integral part of the group.

To accomplish their goals, the Knights introduced new ways to learn tennis, such as video tape and ball machines, week-long (four hours each day) and weekend (six hours a day) clinics in May, and their offshoot, ninety-minute drill groups. The great activity that resulted led to the additional all-weather courts built in 1976, and the necessity to sign up for tennis court times that lasted for a number of years. The Knights employed five assistants one season to help give lessons and run the clinics and programs for the different levels of players participating.

"Tennis night" at the end of the season was the Knight's creation. Previously, there had been a small ceremony, originally at the tennis house before being moved to the Dormie House, to acknowledge the season's winners. Under the

Knights, it grew into a special dinner in the main house, a fun night where everyone got some kind of award. Over two hundred people regularly attended what became one of the special social nights of the year, complete with entertainment and a slide show of the year's happenings. Tennis Night competed with Beach Night for the Labor Day audience so that the departing prep school and college students could participate.

Under the Knights, the men's tennis program grew to include "A" and "B" teams competing in inter-club matches in a league including five other local clubs. The ladies also enjoyed these "social" interclub matches, which involved lunch as well as golf for the ten women on the team.

The women's program was taken into a different dimension in 1985 with the introduction of the U.S.T.A./Volvo matches. These are special team matches sponsored by Volvo and governed by the United States Tennis Association, whereby each player was rated by an outside U.S.T.A. evaluator (with minor input provided by Kit Knight and the club's tennis chair), then promoted or demoted in classification based on a computerized evaluation of her performance. The Volvo was pure competition, with no social trappings, offering the ladies the opportunity to compete on a wider scale. The Creek once fielded five teams of twelve ladies each, but the club's greatest accomplishment was a near miss in the Long Island regionals (the Metropolitan and Eastern regionals might have followed, leading to the

ABOVE LEFT: Harrison and Kit Knight
ABOVE RIGHT: Kit teaching

The Creek 81

ABOVE: Tennis pro Martin Wostenholme
RIGHT: Mag Cullen Broughton, only Creek ladies' champion in three sports

national championships). But even that strong performance locally was considered a great accomplishment for a golf club's tennis team.

By the late 1970s The Creek began to experience a renaissance in tennis to the point where there was a greater balance of membership interest between golf and tennis. This resulted in the club being viewed as a more family-oriented club than in the past. Testament to this was that a majority of the new members of that period were young and played tennis.

The current tennis pro is Martin Wostenholme who came to The Creek from Fisher Island, Florida, in the summer of 1995, succeeding the Knights. His first major change was to discontinue the club's participation in the Volvo tournament (although a few individual members continue to venture "off campus" to

Bill Lewis

Bill Lewis is a club treasure, a devoted employee who has given fifty years of his life to the club. Indeed, The Creek is his life.

Bill currently serves as manager of the clubhouse, but he has always gone beyond his responsibilities, whether they be at the Main Clubhouse, Dormie House, or the Beach to "get it done." Bill is The Creek's "go to" man, the one you enlist to "make it work."

Bill was born in Newport, Rhode Island, in 1928. He made the acquaintance that brought him to The Creek in 1946 while working for his third summer at the Sprouting Rock Club at Bailey's Beach while a high school student. There he met Robert Schumacher, former locker room manager at The Creek. When Creek General Manager Jacob Kramer left after the 1946 season, Schumacher was brought back as his successor, and brought Bill Lewis with him "just for a summer job." Lewis became manager in 1962 upon Schumacher's death.

In 1948 Bill met his wife Anne Chardnet, a Fordham grad who was a receptionist at the Beach. Anne came from Glen Cove, and her father was pastry chef at Piping Rock. They married in 1951, just before Bill was sent to Germany for an eighteen-month tour with the army. He has been at The Creek steadily since his return. Daughters Joanne and Susan were born in 1957 and 1960, respectively, and both have worked as waitresses at The Creek. The Lewis family lived in an apartment on the second floor of the maintenance barn. Anne continued to work at the pool, and over the years acquired a reputation as "mother hen" to the club's youngsters.

Bill and Anne represent the ultimate in dedication and loyalty to The Creek.

---

compete) because the competition proved to be controversial among many of the ladies. He replaced the Volvo program with an intramural league of five teams, selected by their respective captains. This proved very popular, and the idea was extended into the winter season. Wostenholme has also breathed new life into the junior tennis program.

The Summer Camp (former Sports Group) today operates four days per week, combining tennis, golf, sailing, and swimming, with arts and crafts and a play area additional attractions. Although run by a group of college-age counselors under the supervision of a senior counselor, the camp is overseen by a committee of involved mothers.

Jimmy Minsky

ABOVE: Ready to play
RIGHT: Receiving an award from Mrs. Dey

Jimmy Minsky was a beloved member of the club's staff for forty-three years before retiring in 1976. He came to The Creek as a caddie in the late 1920s, and went on to become assistant golf professional, in which capacity he ran the shop and became a very popular teacher, although not an outstanding player himself. In 1930 he was called upon to be the "substitute" caddie for Bobby Jones, and remembered the heat of Jones' stare when he overclubbed him on the 17th hole, and Jones airmailed the green into the cemetery behind.

Minsky also ran the paddle tennis facility in the winter, teaching and arranging games for the members, doing so for a number of years until his retirement in 1976. The Minsky Bowl was a major event on the paddle calendar, held over the Halloween weekend and including a dinner-dance.

Jimmy was a short fellow, with a slight New York accent, somewhat of a character,

With John Pickett III; standing behind are Joseph Dey, George F. Baker, Jr., Henry Harris, Al Seaman, Jim Keresey, and F. C. Smithers.

but in a way that endeared him to people. As a teacher, he relied on colloquialisms such as "get that belt buckle out front." He was an old-fashioned professional, one who minded his parameters, and was seldom seen with the members in the clubhouse.

Jimmy possessed a warm personality, and was terrific with children. He made The Creek a fun place to be. The membership's affection for him, and that of many Piping Rock members, was so great that at his retirement party, Joe Dey was moved to say, "In all my experience around the world, I have never seen such an outpouring of affection." Further testament of this is that to this day his retirement party was the largest ever given for a member of the Creek staff.

Jimmy Minsky passed away in Florida in 1983.

The indoor facility

CHAPTER 12

The Indoor Facility

If any two Board decisions are responsible for the club's sound financial position as it celebrates its seventy-fifth anniversary, they were to build the indoor racquets facility, and to renovate and restore the golf course.

As with paddle tennis, Jim Keresey was the visionary behind the indoor facility. Club president John O. Pickett, Jr. (1980–1983) was the man responsible for making Keresey's dream a reality.

The indoor facility did not receive immediate approval, even though there was a groundswell of interest among the club's racquets players, who sought a twelve-month program at the club. Indeed, the club had a need for an indoor facility to remain competitive with such neighboring clubs as Piping Rock and Nassau, and the possibility had been on the table since being introduced by Keresey in 1963. One third of The Creek's membership, approximately 120 families, had tennis players, and many of them rented time at commercial facilities to play squash or winter tennis.

The indoor racquets facility was formally proposed to the Board by Pickett in February of 1982 as part of a plan that also included building ten new cottages and enclosing part of the Main Clubhouse terrace to create a "Florida Room." Pickett's plan was approved by the Board in January of 1983, albeit minus the cottages, which were vetoed by community opposition.

There was resistance to the indoor facility at first, in fact, a petition was circulated against the proposal. Some felt there was no need for squash at the club; others opposed such a significant investment for a minority of the club's membership. The majority of the membership was supportive, however.

Two issues that caused considerable debate were the location of the building and its architectural style. Two possibilities considered were extensions to the Dormie House, one to the north, the other to the east, with the same brick facade as the other buildings. In the end, though, it was thought best to separate the new structure from the

John Pickett

John Pickett owned the New York Islanders during their four-year reign as Stanley Cup Champions (1980–1983). During his term as Creek president (also 1980–1983), and with Thomas Mullarky as treasurer, Pickett turned the club around financially, and brought the club financial stability, cutting costs to help pay off a quarter-million-dollar mortgage, partly from the operating budget. While membership chairman, he aggressively promoted the club, thereby attracting a large number of new members.

Despite his reputation as a very successful and demanding businessman who preferred quick decisions to consensus-generating meetings, Pickett did not always accomplish the fullness of his visions and plans for The Creek. Otherwise there would be cottages for members alongside the sixth fairway and condos on the Gibson property. Due to unfavorable community reaction, the Board rejected this idea, and it also turned down his proposal to abandon the first five holes and build five new holes near the water on the Gibson property, which Mrs. Gibson had offered to the club at quite an attractive price in the late 1970s. The conservative Board rejected that idea as well (although a portion of the Gibson property opposite the 14th hole was gifted to the club in 1970).

His legacy stands, however, as having brought financial stability to the club at a critical time, facilitating the construction of the indoor racquets complex, and financing the new deck at the Beach Casino.

---

other buildings, placing it down the hill and out of sight, where the more practical steel structure would have less impact aesthetically. The utmost consideration, however, was to produce a first-class facility.

The site for the new building was approved late in 1983, and construction took place during 1984. The price tag was nearly $1 million. The firm of Innocenti & Webel was the architect. The project was financed partly from available funds, the remainder by assessment.

The finished product included two Har Tru tennis courts, two squash singles courts, a squash doubles court, plus a pro shop. The tennis surface was chosen primarily to be consistent with neighboring indoor surfaces (where some members also played) and the club's outdoor surfaces. An artificial surface would have been easier to maintain, but that was only of secondary import.

With the dedicated oversight of Creighton McShane and Jay Wheatley, the facility opened on time and on budget on December 6, 1984, with 350 members in attendance for the ceremonies, which were presided over by President John C. Jansing, and 210 of them remaining on hand for the dinner that followed. The North America Squash Singles Championship was held at The Creek in April of 1985—to rave reviews. The squash courts were quickly rated among the finest in the country.

Under President Bill Kenny's aegis, the squash courts were widened in 1996 after the United States Squash Racquets Association, taking its lead from the international associations, mandated that all recognized tournaments be played on courts with the international dimensions. This meant widening the singles courts by 2 1/2 feet from their existing width, a change that was made

ABOVE LEFT: The tennis courts
ABOVE: Early in construction

easier because of the steel structure of the building.

A Health/Fitness Center was also added to the indoor facility at the same time, responding to the wishes of a large number of health-conscious members. Its success can be measured by the fact that over two hundred members signed up to use the center year 'round. The entire renovation was financed one-third by private donations from squash players (continuing a long-standing Creek tradition), and two-thirds from club funds. The total cost was $540,000.

The indoor facility, and the rehabilitation of the golf course a decade later, together have had a great impact, allowing the club to attract a new vein of young members. Where once tennis was so popular (starting in 1975) that a reservation was a necessity (even though the club did not then, nor ever since, have a "tennis only" membership), today's additional year-round facilities have made life easier. There is no longer a need for reservations at the outdoor courts; members experience little waiting time for getting a court. In the meantime, squash has become one of the most popular sports at The Creek, and reservations for use of the indoor facilities, squash or tennis, are required.

Opening night

The squash singles/doubles courts

The Creek 91

The health/fitness center

Jim Keresey

Although a six-time golf champion at The Creek, no man has had a more profound impact on the club's evolution into the racquets sports than James F. Keresey, a veteran of the Pacific Theater, most notably Iwo Jima, during World War II. Paddle tennis came first, in the 1960s, then squash in 1984, both products of Keresey's vision and persistence.

To recognize Keresey's key role in the evolution of the club's racquets facilities, especially his energy, enthusiasm, and promotion of squash at the club, The Creek inaugurated the James F. Keresey Bowl in 1988 as the trophy for the annual squash member-guest tournament. The first winners of the Keresey Bowl were Jim and his partner, John Havens. The tournament has grown to become the largest squash doubles invitational in the country. Jim also attained a national "Top Ten" ranking in the Veterans' Squash singles and doubles.

Jim Keresey's legacy extends to his presidency (1991–1995), beginning with the renovation of the golf course, the first major revisions to the club's Bylaws, including Board member rotation and full membership for women, with all privileges and equity ownership. The first woman to join The Creek as a full member came in 1993.

Previously, women were able to join, but without equity and voting rights, although allowed to serve on the Board. Widows were placed in a special category called "subscribers." Today, a single woman may join the club with full privileges, and a married couple may designate the wife as the voting member of the family.

The positive impact of Jim Keresey's visions for The Creek will be evident for years to come.

Jim Keresey

Jack Jansing and Jim Keresey at the opening of the indoor facility

The conclusion of a club championship match

94 The Creek

CHAPTER 13

"This Is a Golf Club"

The Creek has always provided a closed, low-key, no publicity environment. The club has eschewed the tournament spotlight, hosting just a small selection of regional championships over the years.

Most likely, the first outside tournament held at The Creek was the 1939 Women's Long Island Amateur. That match-play championship was held for a second time at The Creek in 1956, and then on an almost regular basis in 1961, 1977, 1984, and 1992. The association's (newer) 54-hole medal-play championship was held at The Creek in 1974.

One of the most newsworthy regional tournaments held at The Creek was the 1970 Metropolitan PGA Championship, which was played on October 6-8, seventy-two holes in three days. A field of 120 competed for a share of the $10,000 purse. The course was set up to play at 6,311 yards, and the greens were exceptionally slick.

The tournament was won by Gene Borek, then professional at Pine Hollow. Borek's four-round score of 276 was five strokes ahead of runnerup Mike Fetchik, a forty-eight-year-old former Tour winner, with Craig Shankland, the defending champion, and Billy Farrell tied for third at 283. Former Tour pro Bill Collins was fifth at 285, while Creek's Jerry Pittman and Piping Rock's Tom Nieporte shared eighth place at 288. Pittman lost all chance with a first-round 78.

Farrell fired a course record 64 in the first round, but surrendered the half-way lead to Shankland. Borek assumed the lead with a 65 in the morning round on the final day, his card including eight birdies and a four-putt 6 on the

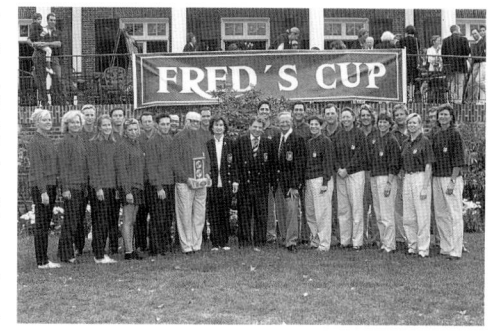

FRED's Cup teams

fifth hole, where he actually took three putts from three feet! He later commented, "I never had a round like that, the greens had me jumpy." Borek closed strong with a 69, including birdies on the 11th, 13th, and 18th holes, hitting the green in 2 on the tournament's ultimate hole.

The WMGA held its (match-play) championship at The Creek in 1972. Despite the summer dates, the contestants were plagued by five days of drizzle, rain, and deluge. The winner was Gwen Straub, wife of Austin Straub, then professional at Huntington Country Club. She defeated "Hatsy" Hart of Baltusrol 5&4 in the finals. The medal round qualified thirty-two women into match play, including medalist Justine Cushing of Meadow Brook, ten-time winner Maureen Orcutt of White Beeches, and one Creek representative, Mrs. Allan A. Ryan. Medal score was 81; a score of 97 qualified.

In 1995 the club hosted the sixth annual French/American Challenge for FRED's Cup, named for the event's sponsor, international jeweler Fred Joallier. The competition was between teams of amateurs, both men and women, representing, on the one hand, the Metropolitan and Women's Metropolitan Golf Associations, and on the other, the Ligue de Paris. The two-day competition, which ended in a 10-10 tie, featured both individual and team competition at match play.

As part of the club's seventy-fifth birthday celebration, The Creek hosted its first major MGA championship, the 1998 Met Open in August, and the Women's Long Island Match-Play Championship in October.

Possibly the most newsworthy "outside" event ever held at the club was a visit on August 20, 1930, by Bobby Jones. At that time, Jones had completed three legs of his Grand Slam. He toured The Creek's course in 68 strokes.

Tom Watson played The Creek in a Pro-Am held for the benefit of Glen Cove Community Hospital. During that event's duration, four clubs shared the role as host, The Creek joining Piping Rock, Meadow Brook, and Nassau in that capacity.

Watson appeared at the invitation of Joe Dey (as did LPGA professional Laura Baugh). At the fourth tee, his former teammate at Stanford, Noel Ryan, son of a Creek member, suggested Tom use a more lofted iron than the one he had chosen. Watson replied, "Rags, I love you like a brother, but please leave club selection to me." Watson proceeded to put his shot a foot below the hole for a birdie 2, then went on to score 67 for his round.

ABOVE: Bobby Jones
RIGHT: Bobby Jones' scorecard

96 The Creek

The Liberty Bell

Perhaps the event of the season for Creek members is the Liberty Bell tournament, an elaborate event held over the July 4 weekend, conducted jointly with Meadow Brook and Piping Rock.

The Liberty Bell started in 1973 as an extravagant member-guest golf tournament in which the club teams play one round on each of the three courses over the weekend, with the final day's host rotating. The event was conceived by publisher Nelson Doubleday (a Piping Rock member) and The Creek's John O. Pickett, Jr.

The golf tournament proved immediately successful, and tennis was added for 1975. The overall concept expanded over the years, and now includes a multitude of sporting contests over the weekend for the wives, children, and house guests of members.

The idea that evolved was that of a family weekend, celebrating the Fourth of July, providing something for everybody—swimming races, trout fishing, shooting, backgammon, bridge, softball, even dog shows—most safely close to home. Awards night, now held annually at Piping Rock, includes fireworks, Scottish bagpipers, and a barbeque. The Creek does entertain its own members with a Fourth of July fireworks display at the Beach, a longtime practice renewed in 1989 when 384 people attended the festivities. (The Liberty Bell fireworks when held at The Creek were staged closer to the main clubhouse, until the year when the wind carried the remnants onto a neighbor's property and littered his pool. As a result, the Awards Night could no longer be held at The Creek.)

The focal point of the Liberty Bell remains member-guest golf tournaments for men and women, as well as ladies' and mixed doubles tennis, and the children's field day. It has become the single biggest country club sporting event in the United States.

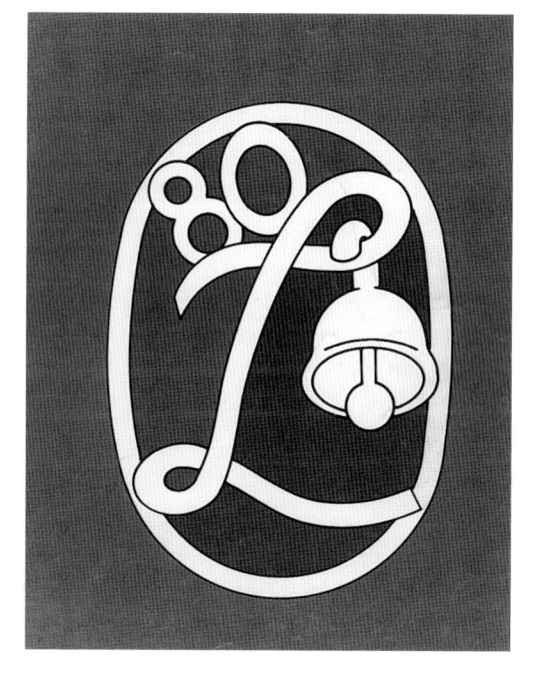

Arnold Palmer appeared at The Creek as a guest of Malcolm McNair and Chase Manhattan Bank, and was a great hit with the members and their children.

Jim Keresey is the only male member of The Creek to have captured club titles in three different sports, having won the golf championship six times, as well as two paddle and three squash doubles titles, in addition to three Keresey Bowl victories. Keresey recalls one golf championship against Ben Milner which "on paper" figured to be relatively easy. Not to take any chances though, Jim went out and birdied the first three holes—only to find himself one-down! Ben also

ABOVE: Stuart Titus
ABOVE RIGHT: Scorecard for Stuart Titus' amateur course record 64
BELOW: The Macdonald Trophy

started "on fire," playing those same three holes in 3-2-3, holing out a nine-iron on the second hole. Jim had to fire a 71 to win. Keresey left his imprint on the 16th hole. The flat rough area to the right of the fairway, often the cleverly-placed destination of his drives, came to be known as "Keresey Gardens."

Former member Stuart Titus, nine times club champ, is the only Creek golfer to date to have challenged for a major regional championship. In 1987 he reached the finals of the Met Amateur at Meadow Brook, where he was defeated by George Zahringer III, the dominant player of that time.

Titus grew up at The Creek—both his father Alan and grandfather Warren were members. Stu was introduced to golf at age ten, with Jerry Pittman his mentor, and first played in the club championship at age eighteen. He became a serious student of the game, and studied the Creek golf course closely for hours at a time. He holds the amateur course record for The Creek with a 64 shot in 1986.

Among The Creek's leading golfers today are the Bodys, Lou IV and V, a notable father and son combination. Lou IV is the 1997 Seniors' champion and for years a strong contender for the men's championship. His son was the Long Island Junior champion of 1988, and also a member of the United State Junior Olympic hockey team at that time. He has won the Creek championship twice. A more recent record-setting performance was the eagle/double-eagle scored on consecutive days by George Holland on the 18th hole at Creek in May 1998.

The Creek is one of seven clubs to participate in the annual Charles B. Macdonald tournament honoring the common architect of their courses. The competition was inaugurated in 1991 by the St. Louis Country Club, the site rotating among Macdonald courses since. The Creek was the host in 1994.

Otherwise, The Creek's only interclub men's competition is with Piping Rock. The club's own golfing calendar, which never had a serious schedule of "trophy tournaments," changed significantly when the Liberty Bell was established as the focal point of the Fourth of July weekend. Prior to the Liberty Bell, the Member-Guest was the "special" event of the year, concluding with a black-tie dinner-dance at the Beach. Its late July date was too close to July 4 to make both events feasible.

The Member-Guest competition was fierce, the Sunday afternoon finals attracting a large gallery, swelled by an influx from the Beach when the match reached the tenth hole. The "guests" ranged from celebrities such as singer Perry Como, who was Bob Townsend's partner, to some of the leading players in the region. Angus Lightfoot Walker wanted to win the Member-Guest badly, and so he often invited two-time British Amateur champion Dick Siderowf as his partner. The far reaches of the left side of the third fairway came to be known as "Siderowf's corner" in honor of his many perfect drives on that hole. They reached the finals one year, only to lose to John Pickett and his partner, Piping Rock's Dick Remsen. One year, Billy Bancroft (also of Piping Rock) drove the tenth green twice in one day.

George Burns, one of America's leading amateur golfers at the time, made his last amateur appearance (as Bill Curran's partner) in the Member-Guest, before turning professional and joining the Tour. In the finals against Fred Williams and Ted Remsen, the Curran-Burns team enjoyed a small lead before Williams sank a 40-foot-birdie putt on 13 and chipped in for a birdie on 14 to even the match. Curran & Burns withstood the challenge, and went on to win the match.

The teams were qualified into flights on Friday, sixteen teams per flight. One year, six teams tied for last two spots in the first flight. With darkness impending, Creek pro Bert McDougall, as referee, decided to have them return the next morning at 6:30 a.m. All twelve players teed off together in the ensuing shootout, and all twelve hit the first green in regulation, prompting one member to observe, "This isn't golf, it's marbles."

At the second hole, one team birdied (to earn its placing), and two others bogied, and were relegated to the second flight. The other three

---

Late Bloomers

Sylvester "Pat" Weaver, former head of NBC and father of actress Sigourney Weaver, took up golf late in life, and played alone until he felt he wouldn't be embarrassed. One day, he returned to the Dormie House and announced in dramatic Shakespearean tones, "Today I suffered the most unfortunate indignity. Today, a foursome went through *me*!"

Edward "Pat" Lenahan, former publisher of *Fortune* magazine, also started late in life, and either played alone or with one friend. One very hot day, he came in "sweating buckets" and commented, "I shot 145, just one of those days when everything went *right*."

Iceberg!

Al Seaman's golf group was called the "*Titanics*" because of a colorful ritual at the 18th hole that set the group apart. Upon reaching the home hole, the team behind could yell "*Titanic*" to double the press bet on the last hole; their rivals could then counter with "Iceberg" to double the bet again.

Mrs. Van Devanter "Muffie" Crisp accepting trophy for New York State Senior Women's Championship

"Muffie" Crisp

For more than half a century, women's golf at the club was watched over by Mrs. Van Devanter "Muffie" Crisp, sixty-three years a member, fifty-nine of these on the Board, first at Women's National, then at The Creek. During these years, Muffie served as Golf, Tennis, and Social chairperson, and was very involved with the club's junior programs. An outstanding golfer, Mrs. Crisp was the first New York State Woman's Senior champion, a title she won in 1953. Her name can also be found on countless lists of winners and top-five finishers for a multitude of Women's National, Creek, Piping Rock, and Women's Long Island Golf Association tournaments over the years.

Muffie's numerous attempts to resign from the Creek Board were always denied until finally she insisted, and the Board acquiesced. In 1987 Muffie was succeeded on the Board by Mrs. William (Jean) Eakins, who has followed in Mrs. Crisp's footsteps with her interest in golf, the Sports Group, bridge, even to overseeing that the brass fittings on the furniture are always properly gleaming. Mrs. Eakins retired from the Board in 1997 when she was named an honorary Board member.

teams halved the third, fourth, and fifth holes, before one team managed a winning par at the sixth. Interestingly, the two "survivors" of the playoff went on to meet in the finals!

The schedule today consists of the President's Cup, once a match-play handicap against par, now contested at medal play with handicaps; the Governors' Cup, the member/member match play championship, best ball of partners, established in the early 1980s; and the Schuyler Nickerson Cup, a mixed best ball medal play handicap on Labor Day weekend.

Late in the season, a group of members once participated in the Cliff Cullen Memorial, a cross-country tournament named for a member who gave the event a certain amount of notoriety. Play started at the second tee, and proceeded to the tenth green, by whatever route chosen. The preferred route was toward the 13th green, from which a free lift to the 14th tee was granted for the final shot across the water. Players carried three clubs and started with three balls, the loss of which resulted in disqualification. Former Creek professional Rick Whitfield held the record for the course with a 9.

As for Cullen, one year he hit his ball atop a tent set up in front of the clubhouse for a wedding reception, and climbed up the flagpole to play his shot. His doggedness and strict adherence to the Rules of golf prompted the Golf Committee to name the contest in his honor.

Women's golf at The Creek reached its apex in the late 1940s and 1950s, a corollary effect to the influx of top women players into the club because of the merger with Women's National.

It was during the fifteen years following the war that The Creek's ladies' golf team was a major force in regional play, winning the WMGA's annual spring team tournament (Long Island division) six times between 1948 and 1962, including the overall regional championship in 1952. In 1949 The Creek boasted seven women with single-digit handicaps, more than any other club in the Metropolitan region, and the highest handicap on the club's "A" team was 5.

Among these top golfers were Mrs. John "Dot" Baldwin, who won the club championship twelve times and was very active as an officer with both the WMGA and WLIGA, and represented the New York region in the Griscom Cup intercity matches; Mrs. Thomas "Dozie" Rudel, a 2-handicapper who came to The Creek from Canada, and to this day has a Long Island Women's Golf Association trophy named in her honor; Mrs. Arthur Atkinson; Mrs. Joseph (Rosalie) Dey; Mrs. Caryl (Harriet) Sayer, who served as president of the WMGA (1951–1952) and represented Long Island in the Triangular team matches; Mrs. Longstreet Hinton; and Martha "Muffie" Crisp. A decade earlier, Grace Amory reached the finals of the WMGA's Championship, where she was defeated by the immortal Maureen Orcutt, a ten-time winner of the event.

As the club's membership evolved toward racquets sports in the ensuing decades, women's golf suffered, but only to the extent that the team today competes in Series 2 of the WMGA's spring competition.

Women's golf at the club includes the 18-hole group and the relatively new (1980) nine-holers, both of which play on Tuesdays, in twosomes to speed play. The niners once played on Thursday mornings over a hybrid course consisting of the first six holes, a shortened 16th, then the regular final two holes so that their round might conclude at the clubhouse.

Next in significance to the "low profile" club championship on the women's annual calendar is the two-day Member-Guest, named in honor of Louise Mills when her husband donated a trophy in her memory for the event.

Among the better players in more recent years have been Pamela Eakins, twice the WMGA Junior champion (1958–1959); Mrs. J. M. Connors and Mag Cullen Broughton, both of

ABOVE: Grace Amory with Maureen Orcutt
RIGHT: Mrs. Balding with her mother, Mrs. Joseph E. Davis, also a Creek member

Arnold Palmer with, from left to right, Mardi Matheson, Pam Eakins, and Jane Keresey

Scorecard for Jerry Pittman's course record 62

The Creek's Golf Professionals

Jack Ross	1923–1939
Bert McDougall	1940–1965
Jerry Piittman	1966–1974
Rick Whitfield	1975–1981
Craig Watson	1981–1988
Jack Druga	1988–1992
John Sanges	1993–

Thanks, But No Thanks

Late in Bert McDougall's tenure at The Creek, he was playing a round with K. C. Li, self-described as the club's worst player, and Nicholas Salgo, who was nearly as unskilled at the Scottish game. When the threesome faced a rain delay on the course, they took refuge in the shelter at the eighth hole. While waiting, Li told Bert, "You know, I've been taking lessons from you for twenty years." Bert responded, "Yes, I know, and please don't tell anyone."

Bert McDougall

whom won the club championship eight times; Jane Keresey, a six-time champion; and Mrs. William Stockhausen. Mag Cullen Broughton is the only woman at The Creek to have won championships in three different sports.

The first golf professional at The Creek was Jack Ross, who served from 1923 through 1939. Ross was an Englishman who, with his family, lived on club grounds in the White cottage.

Ross was succeeded in early May of 1940 by Bernard "Bert" McDougall, a true Scotsman who spoke with a Scottish burr. Bert was born in 1904 and raised in Turnhouse, near Edinburgh where, as a teenager, he learned his golfing lessons while playing hooky from school. He came to the United States in 1920, working as assistant at such clubs as Huntingdon Valley near Philadelphia, Mt. Kisco, and Essex Fells. Ultimately, he enjoyed head professional status at The Creek in the summer and at the Palmetto Golf Club in South Carolina during the winters.

"Mac" is remembered as being devoted to golf and its Rules, a great teacher who was interested in everyone's game. Of all the club's professionals over the years, it was McDougall who took the most interest in junior golf.

McDougall's son Don learned the game and the profession at The Creek, helping his father as assistant professional starting in 1958. He is now the head professional at Shinnecock Hills. While apprenticing at The Creek, the members at times sponsored his junkets on the winter mini tours.

Certainly the most accomplished player among The Creek's golf professionals was Jerry Pittman, who played the Tour occasionally during his years (1966–1974) at The Creek. In 1968 he played in all four majors, finishing tied for seventh in both the Masters and U.S. Open, and tied for twentieth in the PGA (although out of the running in the British Open). He led the Crosby after the first round one year, prompting host Bing Crosby to ask Bob Hope, on national television, "Who's this guy?"

Pittman and Jimmy Wright were far and away the best professionals in the Metropolitan Area during the late 1960s and early 1970s. Pittman won a pair of Met Opens (1965 and 1968), in the latter defeating Wright by eight strokes. He scored 274 for his four rounds, including a new Inwood course record 65 in the third round. Within an 11-hole frame in the final round, Pittman and Wright fired a remarkable 14 birdies at each other!

In local competition, Pittman also captured the 1965 Met PGA, 1967 Long Island Open, 1969 Long Island PGA, and 1969 New York PGA.

Pittman once played the front nine at The Creek in 28, but had to quit to give a lesson. He did establish the (non-competitive) course record at The Creek in 1968 with a 33-29=62 in a casual round with Jim Keresey, among others. Before that round, both Pittman and Keresey complained of poor play, prompting Pittman to give Keresey 10 strokes, a wager Keresey should have won with a fine 73! During the club's Golden Jubilee celebration in 1973, Pittman finished the front nine with five consecutive birdies and seemed poised to challenge his record when he left his drive on the tenth hole far to the right—and wet. He did card a 65, nonetheless, and does hold the competitive course record with a 63.

Pittman was a short driver, a good long iron player, and a fantastic putter. He is also remembered as a good teacher and a "fun guy." He left The Creek for a position at Saucon Valley in Pennsylvania, and while at both clubs wintered at Seminole in Florida, a position he holds to this day.

Between Pittman and the present professional, John Sanges, came Rick Whitfield, Craig Watson (whose father, Bob Watson, was a longtime club professional in Westchester County), and Jack Druga, who apprenticed at Oakmont.

Current professional John Sanges came to The Creek in 1993. His mandate was to provide stability in the pro shop in the face of a tremendous influx of golfers, to be an active teacher, and to strengthen the junior program.

The upstate native came to The Creek a graduate of the highly respected Golf Management program at Ferris State University in Michigan. Many of Sanges' innovations at The Creek thus far are related to junior golf. He has introduced a junior club championship, a parent-child tournament, and has helped organize a ten-club junior league in which The Creek fields a team. He has also helped incorporate golf into the summer camp program, his goal being to have the children on the course at least twice a week, and has put together a junior program for those children who have "graduated" from the summer camp.

John and his staff of two assistant pros and shop manager have remodeled and redecorated the pro shop and upgraded the merchandise sold therein. John has also found time to work on his own game, and in 1997 was one of just three Met Area club professionals to qualify for the PGA Tour's Buick Classic at the Westchester Country Club.

ABOVE: Golf Pro John Sanges
BELOW: Longtime caddiemaster Jim "Googie" Gugliano

Joe Dey

From a golfing standpoint, the most prominent of our members was Joseph C. Dey, Jr., who served the United States Golf Association with distinction as executive secretary during the years 1934 to 1968, then became the first commissioner of the Tournament Players Division of the PGA from 1968 to 1973. Dey was elected to the World Golf Hall of Fame in 1975, the same year he became the second American ever to be named captain of the Royal & Ancient at St. Andrews. The following year, he received the Distinguished Service Award from the Metropolitan Golf Association, to go with the Gold Tee Award he had received from the Metropolitan Golf Writers in 1966.

As part of Dey's induction as R&A captain, he was asked to "play himself in" by hitting a ceremonial drive off the first tee, accompanied by a cannon blast—a daunting task for just an average player whose handicap never was better than 15. That season at The Creek, Dey was often seen on the practice tee, driver in hand, perfecting his stroke, so that he might hit an acceptable shot at St. Andrews in the fall. This was one instance when practice did make perfect.

Joe Dey

In the world of golf, Joe Dey was a man whose name was synonymous with such accolades as "class," "integrity," "diplomacy," "reliability," "good judgment," and "tradition." Jack Nicklaus once said of him that he "set the tone for dignity and fair play" in tournament golf. He was a very proper, polite, and formal person.

Joe Dey was born on November 17, 1907, in Norfolk, Virginia, and considered becoming a minister early in life, a possibility that prompted one member to speculate, "Had he become a minister, Who would have been working for Whom?"

Joe's father was an avid sportsman, a college football player, in fact, and kindled his son's interest in sports. While a collegian at the University of Pennsylvania, he worked as a sports reporter for a local newspaper, then became involved with a golf magazine. In that capacity, he followed Bobby Jones throughout the 1930 U.S. Amateur at Merion, last leg of the Grand Slam, and consequently made the acquaintance of several USGA officials.

When Joe assumed his position with the USGA, he worked from a small office in Manhattan. But he took a strong personal interest in all aspects of USGA work, doing what he could to take the burden off the shoulders of the volunteers, and quickly his own work multiplied, and his reputation grew.

Perhaps the high point in his career with the USGA was his role in the unification of the USGA and Royal & Ancient

ABOVE: Rosalie Knapp
LEFT: Joe and Rosalie Dey at Golf Awards Night 1988

versions of the Rules of golf. He started *Golf Journal*, the official mouthpiece of the USGA, worked on the amateur code, and developed the roping system for galleries at the 1954 U.S. Open at Baltusrol. As a tournament official, it fell upon his shoulders to disqualify apparent winner Jackie Pung for signing an incorrect scorecard in the last round of the 1957 U.S. Women's Open at Winged Foot. Joe always advocated contesting the U.S. Open in three days, with 36 holes on the final day, even after the near collapse of Ken Venturi at Congressional in 1964, and it was Joe who was primarily responsible for toughening up the host course for the Open.

Dey's wife, the former Rosalie Knapp, and her mother were prominent among the members at the Women's National. Rosalie came from a golfing family—she was the daughter of Edward S. Knapp, an accomplished player and frequent competitor in the Met Amateur. Rosalie herself was an accomplished player, and served a term as president of the Women's Metropolitan Golf Association (1935–1937).

Joe Dey's role at The Creek did not have the level of prominence of his national involvement. He did serve on the (at times consolidated) Golf, Green, and Grounds Committees (a "distinct honor," he always said), from 1959 until resigning in 1986, although his cost-conscious approach to course maintenance may have impacted the conditioning of the golf course over time. Nonetheless, his reputation at The Creek was such that one youngster knew of him as "The Golf Chairman of the whole wide world."

Joe Dey was a charming, gracious gentleman, although often autocratic and uncompromising when it came to golfing matters. He passed away on March 4, 1991. He was elected posthumously into the Golf Hall of Fame the following year. Part of his legacy at The Creek is the Joe Dey Trophy, awarded to the winner of the men's club championship.

"The view"

CHAPTER 14

The Golf Course Restoration

The Creek golf course had steadily declined over the years, a consequence of good and bad times, and a byproduct of a cost conscious sequence of Boards and Green Committees influenced for many years by Joe Dey. Joe always looked upon St. Andrews as the ideal golf course, and to him that meant "natural," consequently low maintenance.

During the years 1968 to 1978, a number of "unnecessary" bunkers were removed from the course, and this impacted the character of the design, as architects such as Geoffrey Cornish, Ben Crenshaw, and Tom Doak have pointed out. During this time, less and less was done to maintain the course. This trend followed approximately thirty years of superb conditioning, the years, starting in the early 1930s, that Jock Dishington held sway as green keeper. Dishington retired in 1966.

Steve Dickey, who was appointed green keeper in 1974, served the club for twenty years, the last fifteen as general manager. He played a significant role in the rejuvenation of the facilities, purchasing modern course maintenance equipment, personally overseeing repairs to the buildings, and computerizing the restaurant, all on a minimum budget. The later years of Dickey's tenure coincided with the presidency of Richard C. Meyer (1987–1991), a time when the club was mostly occupied with long-neglected infrastructure problems, most prominently the golf course. The recession of this period added to the financial pressures, mandating the club's cost control policies.

Our present manager, Robert Stein, Beach manager at the time, succeeded Dickey in 1993 when Steve left to become manager at Whitemarsh near Philadelphia. Steve passed away in 1996.

Nonetheless, despite Dickey's valiant efforts, problems remained unsolved. By the late 1980s, the course was plagued by agronomical problems that prevented either water or air from properly permeating the ground. Joe Dey brought Bill Jones in from Merion late in 1987 as superintendent, but despite his efforts, the course restoration was still necessary.

Tom Doak on The Creek

In his recent book, *The Confidential Guide To Golf Courses,* Tom Doak included The Creek in a special international listing of his favorite courses, called "The Gourmet's Choice: 31 Flavors of Golf." Here are a few of his comments:

". . . it's very difficult to single one (Raynor course) out as a favorite, but I've picked The Creek because it has made such a stirring comeback.

". . . as you cross the club's drive to the sixth tee, the golf takes a sudden turn for the dramatic. The sixth is one of the wildest holes in my acquaintance, sharply downhill with its punchbowl green tucked away to the left, a deep bunker at the front right, and a narrow berm surrounding all but the front left entrance. The straight approach over the bunker is daunting, but a perfectly judged shot to the left will be carried into the middle of the green by its pronounced tilt. From here in, it's great golf, with several dramatic two-shotters.

"All in all, the course is a bit short in length, but long on character."

In 1992, spearheaded by President Jim Keresey and the club's Executive Committee, and motivated by the realization that the course was no longer what it once was (in fact, the possibility of losing all 18 greens was imminent!), the club assessed each member $4,000—the largest assessment in the club's history—despite resistance from some Board members and general members as well. As a result of this courageous decision, the club spent $1.7 million to renovate and restore the golf course, including a state-of-the-art irrigation system that replaced one that had served the club for thirty years. The major component of the golf course project was a restoration of the course to the original Macdonald concept, and for this purpose youthful architect Tom Doak and his very capable assistant, Gil Hanse, were brought aboard to address four major concerns. (Doak had just recently completed a very successful restoration at Piping Rock, working under Pete Dye, and was Garden City Golf Club's consultant on matters pertaining to course restoration.)

The concerns Doak and Hanse addressed were plentiful. Over the years, because of routine maintenance practices, the greens had become impenetrable below three inches, and as a result were dangerously at risk. Also, many of the greens had shrunk, and two (the 14th and 18th) had lost their original shape. Of the course's original 110 bunkers, fewer than 60 remained, and many of those had lost their size or shape. The tees, built in the 1920s, were inadequate in size for the amount of play of the 1990s, which was quadruple the original volume. And a number of trees and wild underbrush had been allowed to grow on the course, at times disturbing the view of the Sound, and also, at times, interfering with circulating wind currents often necessary to refresh the greens as well as bolster the challenge of the course.

Doak and Hanse redesigned all the tees and greens, enlarging many of them, and restored the bunkers to their original look—grassy faces, with sand at the bottom only, a Macdonald signature. More than twenty abandoned bunkers were restored. The course was effectively closed, except for some limited play of designated holes, from August of 1992 through the late Spring of 1993 while the work was carried out—set back some by a severe nor'easter in late fall of 1992.

The formal reopening of the course, together with the celebration of the club's seventieth anniversary, took place on Memorial Day weekend. The revitalized course was extremely well received by the general membership, who now play it in such large numbers that a marshal is often required. A representative of the USGA Green Section, upon seeing the outcome of the renovation, commented that the project, "was one of the most ambitious I have ever seen, and succeeded beyond anything I would have expected!"

The success of the project rested in the hands of many, such as Jim Keresey, Bill Holmberg, Tom Parker, and especially a diligent Oversight Committee, chaired by Bill Kenny and comprised of Bob Gardner, Jack Thomas, Don Sutherland, Dana Winslow, Peter Karches, and Holmberg. This committee met a total of thirty-four consecutive Saturdays to insure compliance with budgets, timetables, and quality. Finally, on September 1, 1997, as an effort to maintain the quality of the new greens, the Board voted to ban the use of steel spikes.

The result of all these efforts is a course that *Golf Digest in 1997* has rated sixth best in the country in terms of conditioning.

The club has, during the winter of 1997–1998, commenced a program, under the direction of architect Gil Hanse, designed to improve the cart paths. One goal of the project is to control the flow of the carts, directing traffic away from the greens, whose perimeters had become worn. The program was also instigated for safety reasons, because the existing paths often traversed rocks or tree roots, and were quite bumpy.

Curiously, Creek golf has benefited indirectly from the indoor racquets facility since many of the new members it attracted were also golfers. In addition, since the club's traditional tennis players helped pay for the golf course restoration, many of them decided to try the game, and liked it. Many of the more senior tennis players also found that the game took less of a physical toll than tennis. And so, the golf course today is more active than it ever has been.

As a result, for the first time ever the club established a "cap" on full members at 400, including summer guests, as well as various other weekend playing restrictions, all designed to accommodate overcrowding on the golf course.

Renovating the greenside bunker at the second hole

LEFT: The O'Rourke Resthouse

"The Shadow President"

During an era when many of the club's presidents were Manhattan-based businessmen, managing club affairs became so demanding as to require day-to-day attention—and who was better equipped to assist than Innis O'Rourke, Jr., who not only lived and worked locally, but was more than happy to provide such oversight. So much, in fact, that he quickly earned the unofficial title of "Shadow President," a title he carries with pride to this day.

Like his father, Innis has had a distinguished career of service to the club, including stints as secretary, golf, green, and Beach chairman over the years. He was also largely responsible for a most welcome recent addition to the Creek golf course—the Innis O'Rourke Resthouse at the eighth tee!

The Seventieth Anniversary Celebration

The club's seventieth anniversary in 1993 coincided with the reopening of the restored golf course, giving the membership two reasons to celebrate. Although not as elaborate as the fiftieth anniversary celebration, there were nonetheless golf, tennis, and softball tournaments. The black-tie party took place on Memorial Day, replacing the annual "Open the Beach" party, under a large pink and white tent set up on the front lawn, with vintage automobiles from the 1920s lining the circle.

Two highlights of the festivities were the formal presentations of two awards for outstanding accomplishments. The first presentation by President Jim Keresey of a Steuben glass sculpture was to Bill Holmberg who, perhaps more than anyone else, was responsible for galvanizing attention to the golf course problems and helping to mobilize the necessary resources to solve these problems. The fruits of his efforts—and those of many members—were clearly evident on this opening weekend for the *new* Creek golf course.

The second presentation of a Steuben piece by Jim Keresey was to Anne and Bill Lewis in recognition of Bill's forty-five years of dedicated service to the club, shared with and supported by his lovely wife. It is remembered that Bill was especially fond of the microphone provided him to say a few words for the occasion—and he regaled his audience with many anecdotes and warm sentiments accumulated over the years.

The Croquet Lawn

As part of the golf course project, a croquet lawn was installed in the unused area between the clubhouse and sixth tee. Construction started in the fall of 1992, and the first game was played the following Spring on what is now recognized as the finest croquet lawn on the East Coast. Funds from voluntary contributions covered 80 percent of the cost.

American Rules Six Wicket Croquet was introduced to The Creek by member and Croquet Chairman Bill Whitman, who caught the "croquet bug" that summer at Newport. Croquet professionals have been imported annually to introduce the membership to the sport, whose following now numbers approximately one hundred. Annual tournaments are held with both Piping Rock and Seawanhaka-Corinthian Yacht Club. The first club championships were staged in 1996, with Heather and Randy Bartholomew winning the doubles and Randy the singles.

The Creek in Color

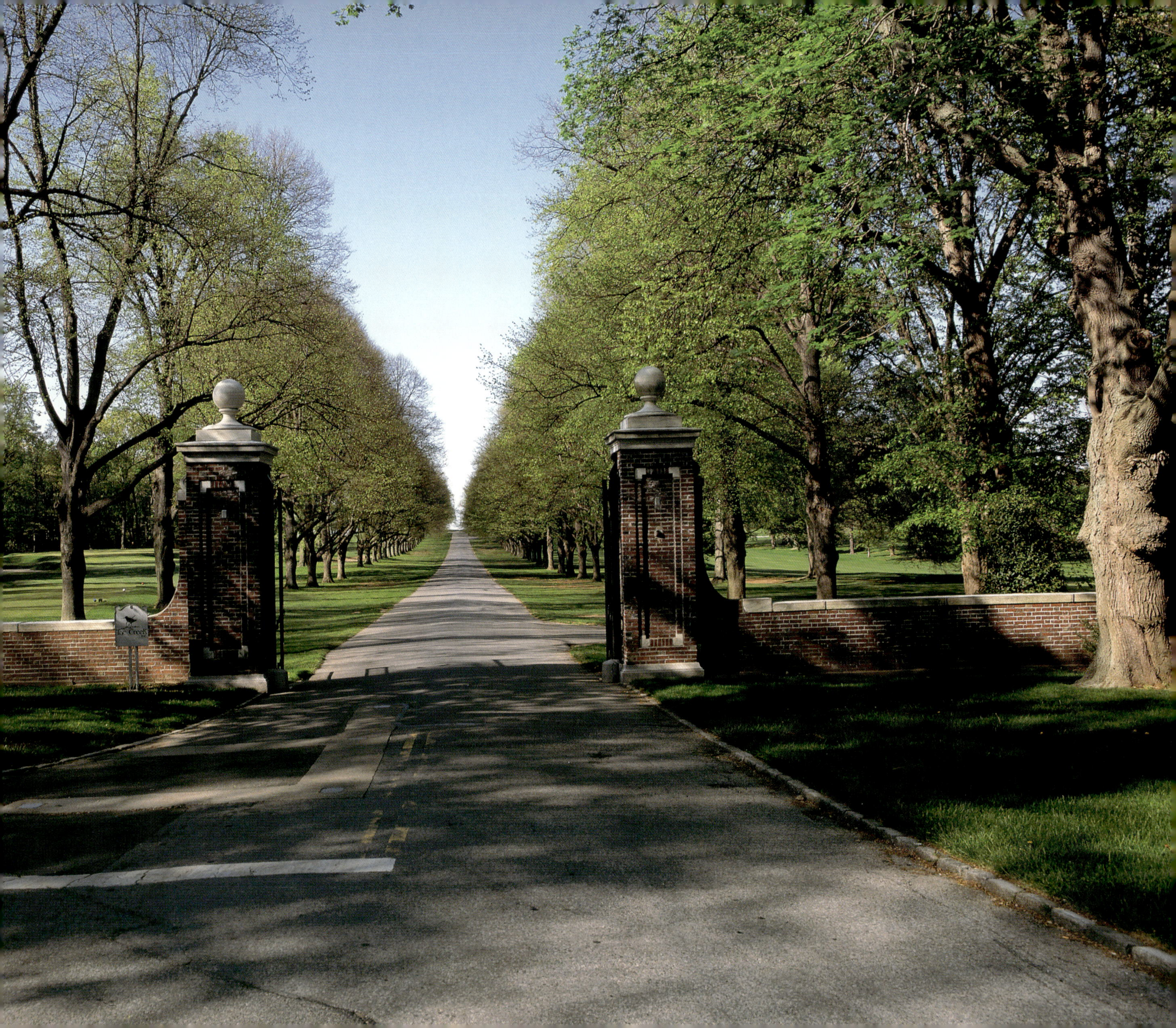

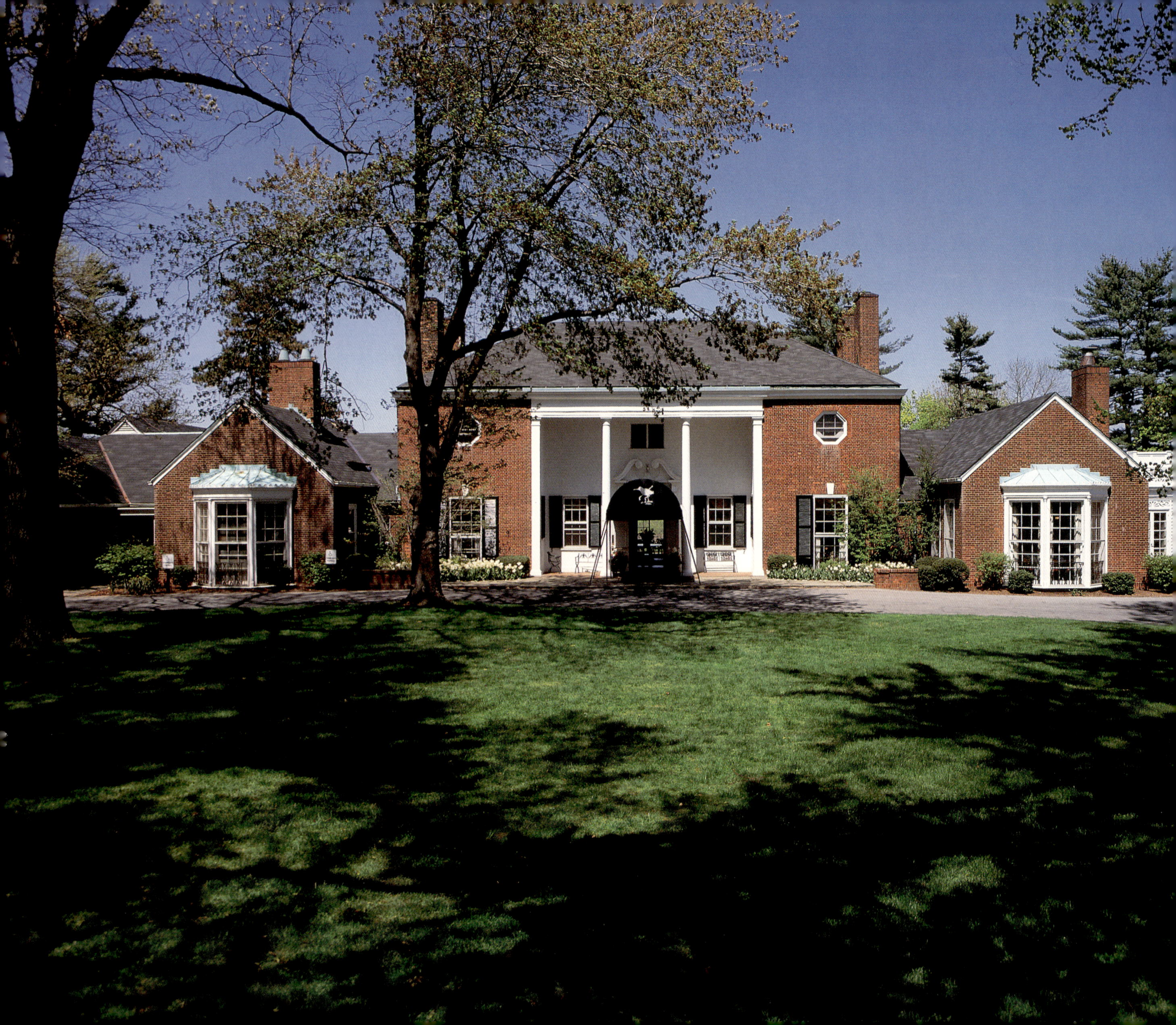

The main lounge

The main lounge

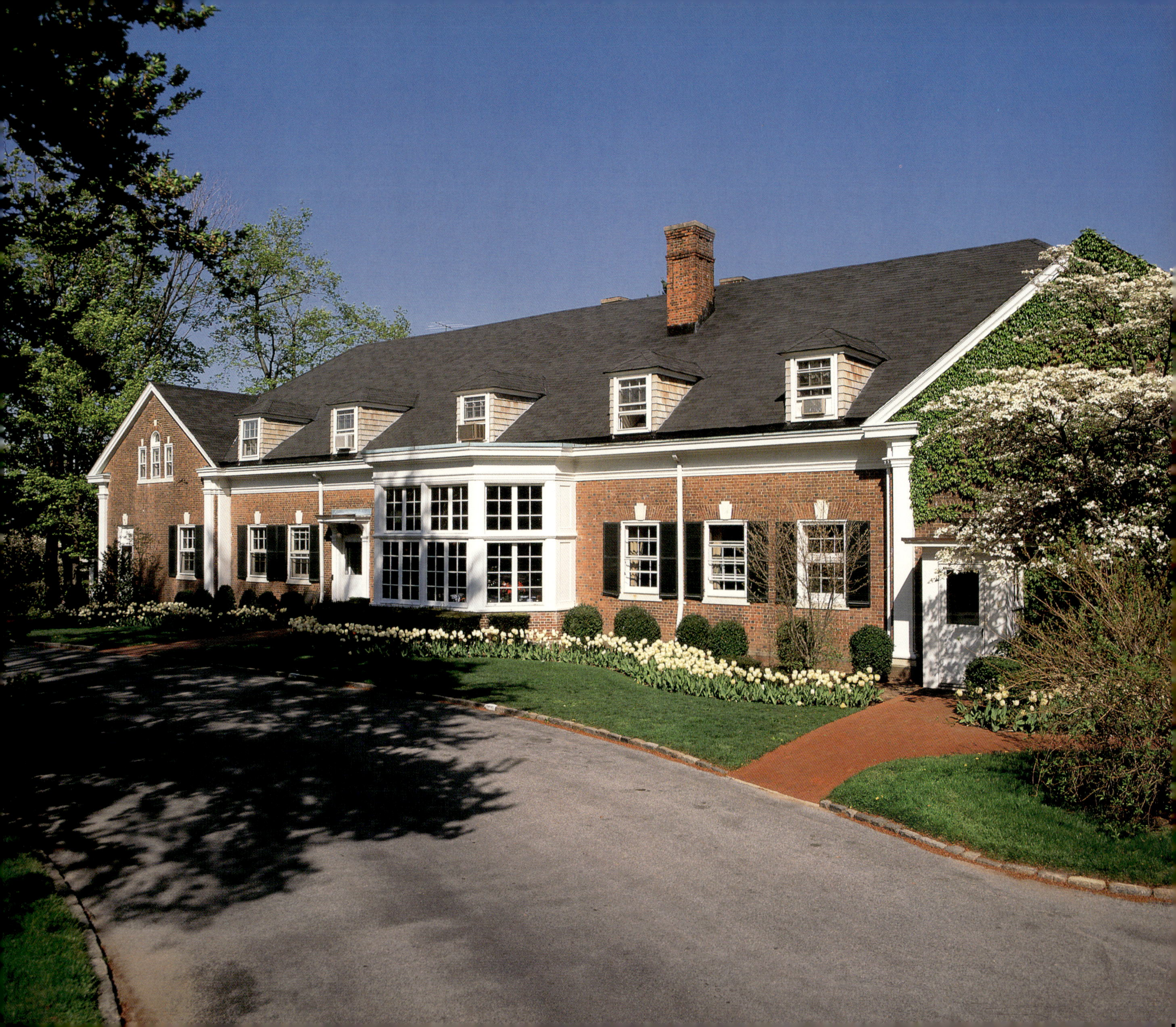

ABOVE: Seventieth Anniversary Dinner Dance
RIGHT: Long Island Symphony Orchestra concert on clubhouse lawn

118 The Creek

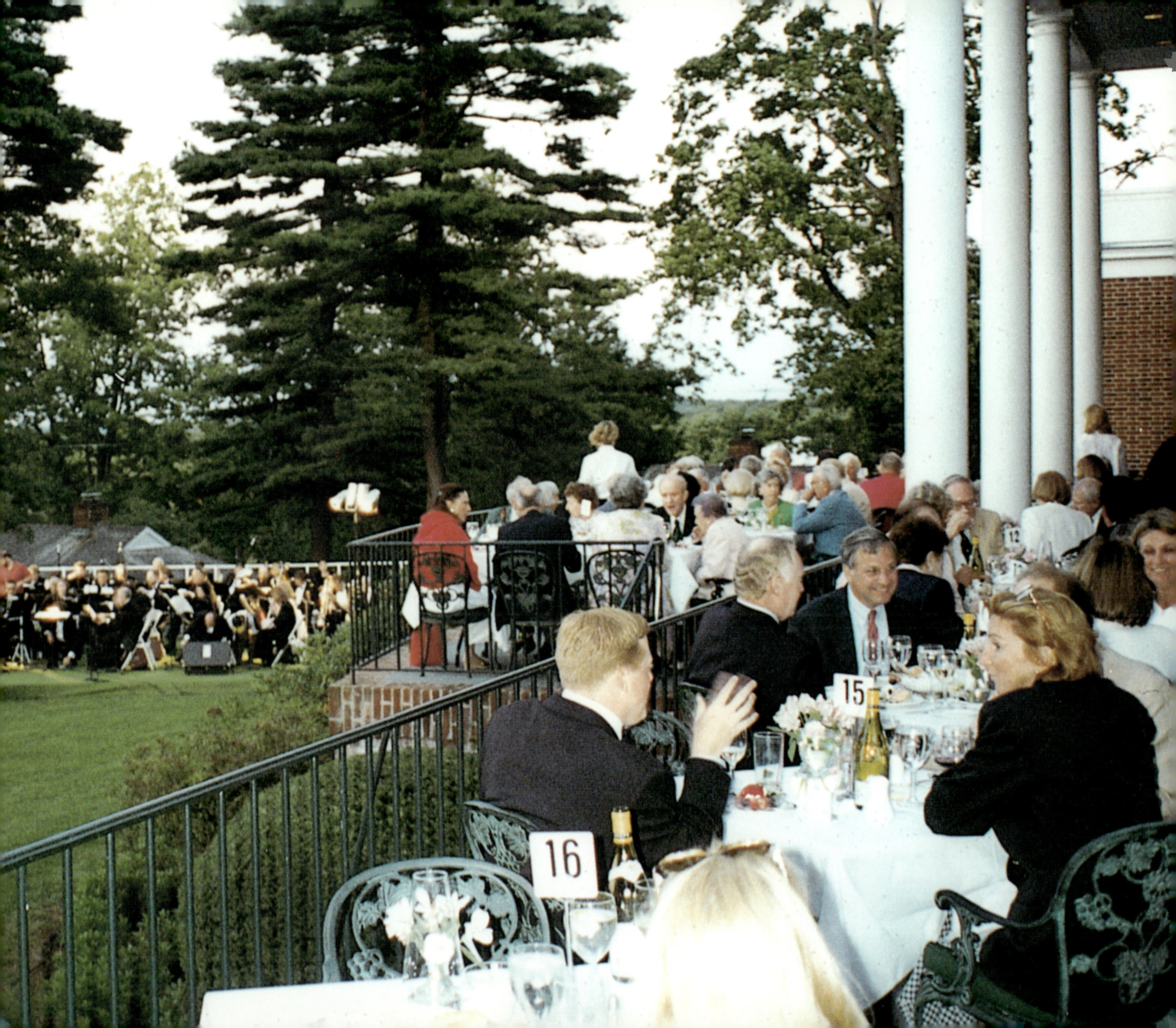
15
16

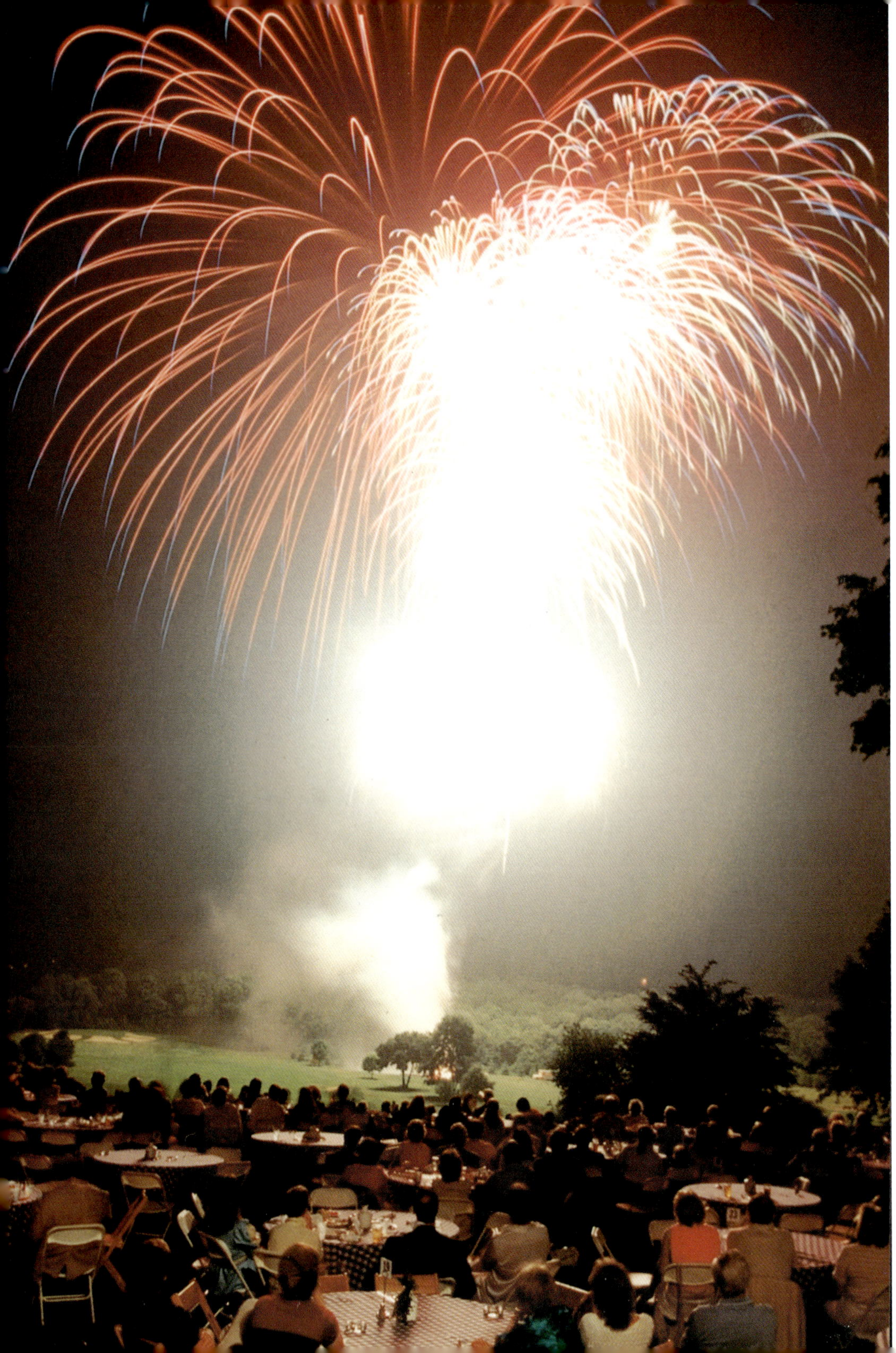
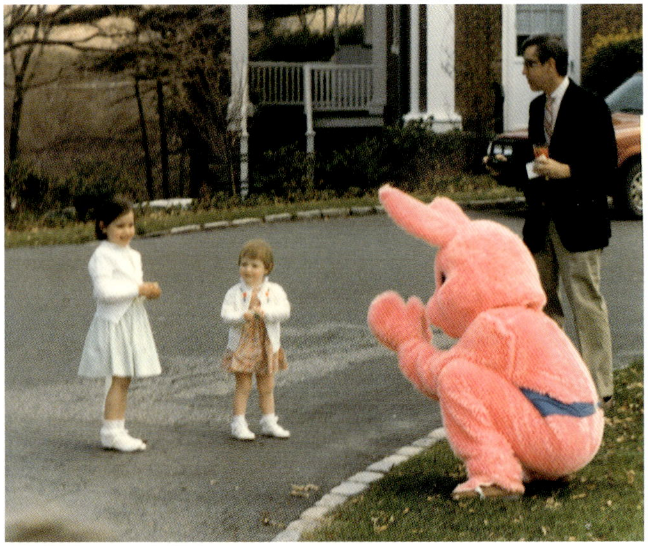
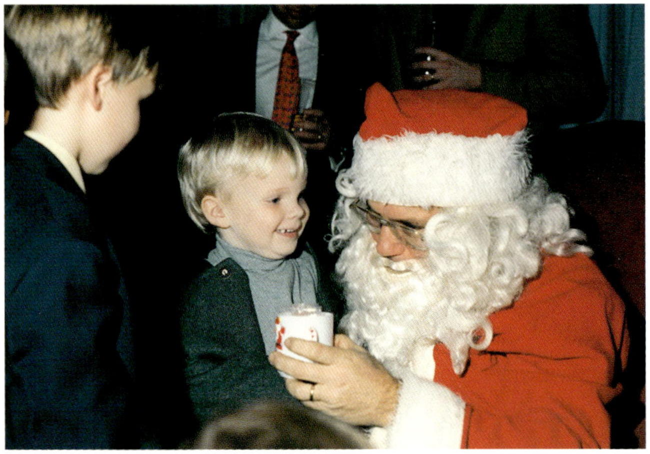

Here follows a hole-by-hole description of the course.

Aerial view looking north

LEFT: The opener plays to a blind fairway, preceded by mounds, that rolls downhill beyond the drive zone to a pair of cross bunkers about 60 yards from home. The entrance to the green, and the putting surface itself, both fall sharply to the left. The greenside bunker to the right is set down below a high mound, and there is a sharp falloff to the left of the green. Upon playing this hole, one immediately recognizes the Macdonald imprint, which is hardly apparent at all on the next two holes.

RIGHT ABOVE: The second fairway is preceded by a bunker left and flanked by another to the right of the landing area. The approach to the green must contend with three bunkers to the right, one 30 yards ahead of the green, and another pair on the left. The putting surface is relatively small, and is divided left to right by a medium-sized crown.

RIGHT: The third hole presents a narrow target off the tee, with a row of Linden trees parading in line along the right side of the hole, bordering the club's quarter-mile entrance road. A bunker 160 yards from home guards the right side of the drive zone, and there are mounds in the left rough. The hole rises moderately into another back-to-front green that is bunkered left and twice right.

The fourth is an "Eden" par 3, modeled after the 11th hole at St. Andrews. Its tee is set back in a chute of trees. There is a bunker 30 yards ahead of the green on the left, another at the left side, two more on the right, and the green is circled behind by a long, narrow bunker. The right-front and left-side bunkers act as a team, narrowing the entrance to the green while at the same time, each preventing a safe shot away from the other.

Last of The Creek's "Parade Grounds" holes, the fifth doglegs slightly to the left beyond the drive zone, then plays uphill to the green. The row of Lindens stands watch over the right side of the hole through the landing area, which is bunkered on the left. The back-to-front putting surface is protected by bunkers well below its left and right sides, the latter cutting across the entrance.

ABOVE AND RIGHT: From the sixth tee the golfer can enjoy one of the most breathtaking views in Met-area golf, with both Greenwich and Stamford in sight across the Sound. The hole plays from a tee elevated far above its tumbling fairway, with woods along the left and a bunker right. The fairway drops abruptly about 120 yards from home, then rises once again before falling into the punch bowl green, which is set behind a huge, high-mounded bunker across its right front. The putting surface itself falls away from the approach, from the left front to the right side, and also breaks considerably away from the left side.

126 The Creek

ABOVE: The par-5 seventh hole demands a good carry over rough to reach a fairway that rises through the drive zone, with waist-high fescue grass and fairway bunkers on both sides. Beyond that point, the hole falls abruptly, with a bunker on the left side of the fairway 150 yards from the green hidden from view on the second shot. The slightly-elevated green is bunkered twice at either side.

The Creek 127

ABOVE: The eighth is a Redan hole, with the green set on a left-to-right angle to the tee, behind a relatively-mild, albeit large, Redan bunker across its right front. The putting surface rolls from left to right as well as front-to-back. Two deep bunkers hidden from the tee guard the left side.

LEFT: The ninth is a good-sized par 4 with its green elevated some 30 feet above the fairway. Two bunkers guard the left entrance to the fairway, and the rough off to the right is sand-based. The approach to the green must carry a pair of fescue-adorned mounds and a large bunker. The putting surface breaks back to front, with a dangerous falloff behind.

With the tenth hole the golf course reaches the Beach, which parallels the left side of the fairway from drive zone to green. The hole is of the "Cape" genre, with the drive calling for a carry over an inlet that crosses the fairway on a left-to-right angle. The pitch to the green (at bottom of picture) must contend with a large bunker across the left front. The putting surface falls left to right, and there is a dangerous drop-off to the right into a series of bunkers.

LEFT AND FACING PAGE TOP: The 11th hole island green measures over 80 yards front to back, and is surrounded by the inlet. The hole is bunkerless, and the green relatively flat, with a small swale through its center. The hole is of the Biarritz genre, first imported to the United States at Piping Rock (number 8) before reaching its ultimate expression as the ninth at Yale.

FACING PAGE BOTTOM: The fairway on the 12th hole is an island of green surrounded by patches of sandy rough on either side. One bunker protects the right side of the drive zone. The small green is surrounded by six smallish traps, which leave but a very narrow entrance at the front. The putting surface is canted from the left rear down toward the right front corner.

The Creek 131

LEFT AND ABOVE: The 13th and 14th holes are the backbone of the golf course, two imposing par 4's back to back. The 13th turns nearly 90 degrees to the right beyond the drive zone, leaving all but the longest hitters with a long carry over a forest of reeds to a green bunkered twice on the right. The tee is slightly elevated, and there is a bunker to the right of the landing area. The inlet parallels the left side of the hole from the dogleg home.

RIGHT: Much of the fairway of the 14th hole is hidden from sight at the tee by tall reeds, which demand a do-or-die carry. The hole bends right, with more reeds beyond the corner. Frost Creek crosses the hole about 130 yards from home, from which point the fairway rises to an elevated back-to-front green bunkered once well below the right side, and once at green level to the left. The "Creek bird" on the club"s logo inhabits the marshes on this hole.

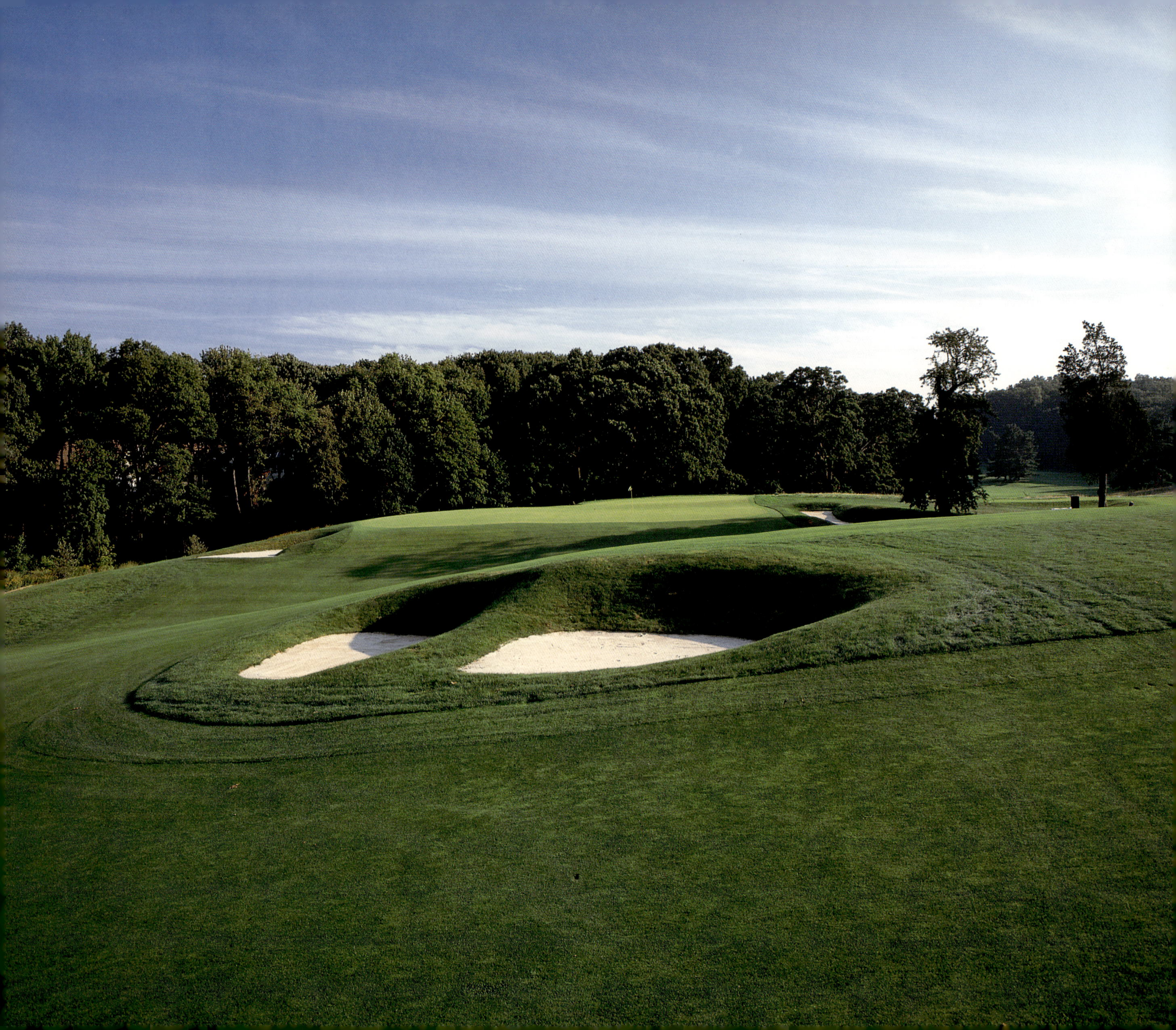

LEFT: With the 15th hole the course leaves the Beach area and heads back toward the clubhouse. The 15th plays to a large tumbling fairway that falls off sharply to the left, with bunkers angling across the fairway further ahead. Just short of the green is a large gully which gathers all shots that fall short of the putting surface. The green is shaped like a backwards "L," with a shelf on the back right sector. Bunkers guard the left and right edges.

ABOVE: The tee at the 16th offers a panoramic view from well above fairway level. The drive zone is flanked by bunkers 220-240 yards from the tee, and there is a third bunker falling into the fairway from the left about 75 yards from home. The elevated green is two-tiered, raised at the back, and is bunkered at both sides. The hole was named "Oak" after the tree to the left of the fairway, which is believed to be the third oldest oak tree on Long Island.

RIGHT: The 17th is the familiar "Short" hole common to all Macdonald courses. The table-top green is perched above two bunkers that guard its left, right, and front flanks. There is a dangerous falloff behind, and the putting surface tilts from back to front.

The Creek's home hole, a short par 5, gives a deceptively wide-open look off the tee, although the fairway itself is a rather narrow band that is bunkered short of the landing area on both sides. From there the hole plays straight uphill to the green, which is set in front of the clubhouse. A second bunker some 75 yards from home on the right side threatens the average player's second shot. The two-tiered green slopes back to front, and is guarded by two bunkers on the left side. A shot that falls short on the right side, or an overly-aggressive putt from the upper tier, may leave the golfer with a recovery from 25 yards in front of the green.

Aerial view looking south

Summer at the Beach

138 The Creek

The Creek 139

140 The Creek

The Creek 141

142 The Creek

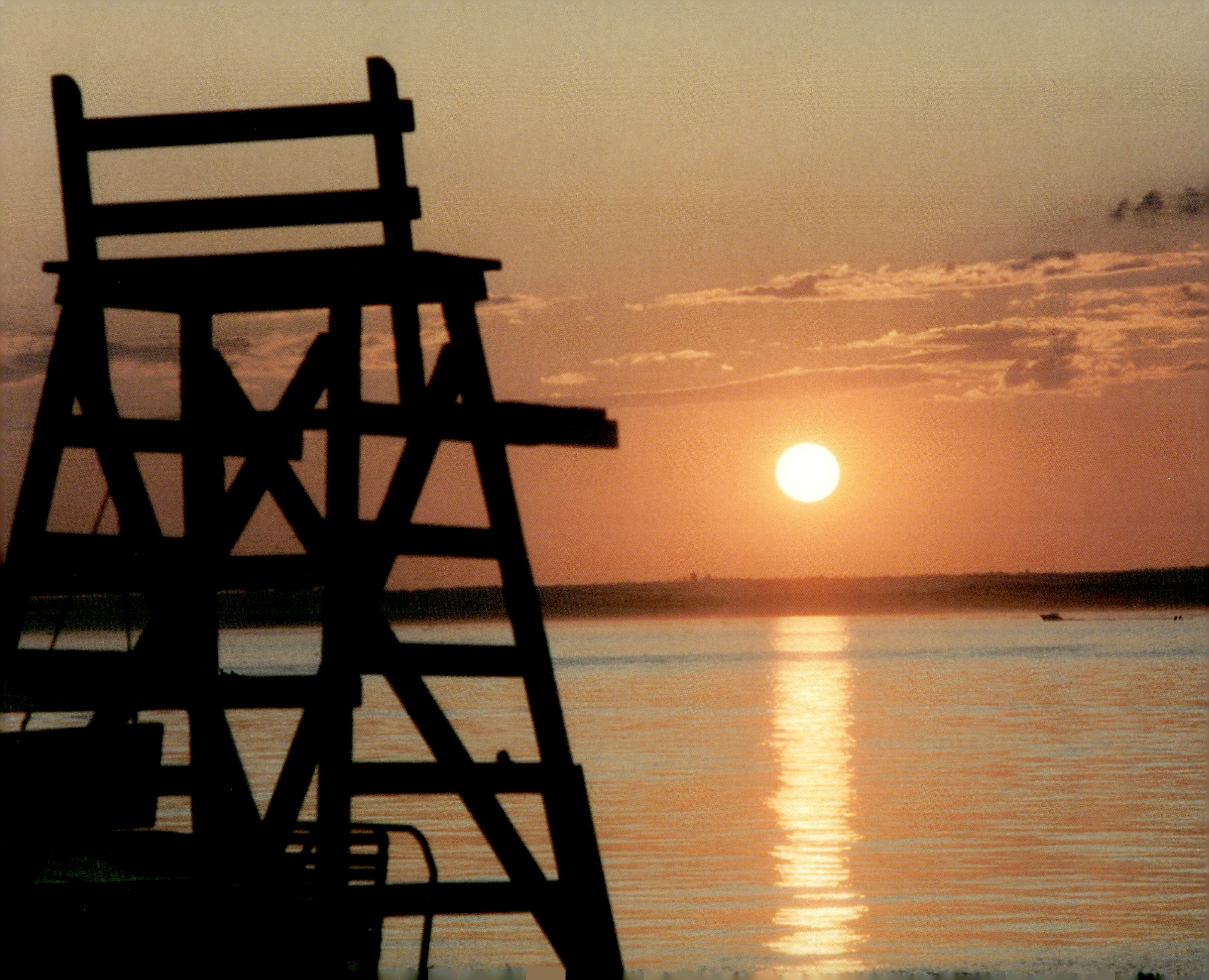

The Pine Room today as a dining room

CHAPTER 15

The Gold Coast, Revisited

The "Gatsby Era" ended with the Depression, but the Gold Coast remains as one of the more affluent regions in the Northeast. Gatsby's descendants today would find a far more sedate social life, in general, although club life at The Creek and Piping Rock might, in some small ways, resemble the lifestyle of the twenties.

The Creek, indeed the entire Gold Coast, faced a serious, potentially devastating, crisis in the late 1960s when Robert Moses, Governor Nelson Rockefeller's parks commissioner, aggressively advocated a bridge connecting Oyster Bay with Rye, New York. Moses' proposed access roads to the bridge would have destroyed both the Creek and Piping Rock properties. The clubs and the surrounding communities, led by Creek member Martin Victor and guided by club president William S. Renchard, devised a quite ingenious solution that included The Creek deeding its land under the Sound and surrounding Frost Creek to the federal government, thereby bringing the property under the protection of environmental laws. This was a key component of a plan which ultimately led to the defeat of the Oyster Bay bridge.

The clubhouse has evolved and expanded over the years. The first major change in the postwar years was the addition of the Gibson Room in 1954 as a comfortable place to socialize near the popular bowling alleys. The Gibson Room included a bar, and offered semi-formal dining (jackets required). Previously, the club had provided a small portable bar in a corner of the Lounge, which later was moved to the hallway next to the bowling alleys.

At the conclusion of William Renchard's presidency in 1970, the kitchen was moved upstairs from the basement to the east wing, next to the formal paneled dining room. Previously, a dumbwaiter had carried the food upstairs to a staging area in what is now the Breakfast Room.

Al Seaman, club president from 1975 to 1980, played a significant role in molding The Creek as we know it today. Known as "The Great

Bill Casey's "Foursome"

CIA director Bill Casey was a Creek member, and his every round at the club posed a disruptive logistical problem. Casey arrived either in a caravan of dark blue limousines carrying the many agents who were to guard him, or by helicopters. His rounds were an orchestrated procession of a single player surrounded by agents carrying golf bags (holding machine guns), but not playing golf. Other groups on the course were paced two holes ahead or behind Casey.

On one occasion, a woman on horseback suddenly appeared from the direction of the tennis house. Quickly she was surrounded by agents who appeared from behind trees. She was restrained, questioned, and escorted down the driveway, then finally released when Casey was at a safe distance.

The formal dining room

Communicator" (he was president of a major advertising agency), he was elected to the Board to be a catalyst, to open communications between the membership and what was considered an incommunicative Board. Subsequently, as house chairman and later, as president, Seaman instituted many innovations, such as Friday Night Specials, to stimulate greater member activity at the club, and he maintained consistent communication with the membership about what was happening at their club.

During the winter and spring of 1994 the clubhouse terrace was expanded in a semicircle out toward the 18th green, and stairs were relocated on both sides. This provided much more room for comfortable outdoor dining, and a spectacular setting for an event such as a wedding reception or a concert. In fact, few members' daughters have foregone the opportunity to hold their wedding reception in such a spectacular setting, overlooking the 18th fairway and looking toward Long Island Sound.

In 1997 the building was expanded southerly to provide a more attractive, direct access to the Gibson Room. Included was a beautifully decorated foyer with a coat room, an expanded men's room, and a new ladies' room.

The membership at The Creek has a low tolerance for repetition and a strong preference for novelty. The club holds a black tie affair every few years, a sharp contrast with the 1950s, when there were several each season. And whereas the parties of that era lasted well into the morning hours, nothing of the sort is true today. The social highlight of the year is the "Open the Beach" dinner dance. The members enjoy an occasional outdoor concert on the sloping lawns behind the clubhouse.

What "made" the club socially from the war years into the 1970s were the buffets, Thursday nights ("maid's night out") in the clubhouse and both Saturdays and Sundays at lunchtime, mostly in the winter. The Sunday buffets were once very elaborate and elegant, featuring lobster and shell fish, and lasted from noon until 4 p.m. Members came out to the club from New York

City, many by chauffeured limousine, then returned home after the buffet. The Saturday buffet was stopped in the late 1950s and replaced by a Friday night buffet at the Beach in the summer.

Eventually, the niceties of the buffet were scaled down as the club became less formal and more cost conscious, eliminating some extravagances. Attendance at the buffets dwindled, all the more so as a new generation of members became diet conscious. As interest waned, most of the weekly buffets were held in the main clubhouse for economy, then stopped altogether by the late 1970s, replaced by a la carte menus. Today the club offers buffets on the major holidays (except Christmas), and on special occasions at the Beach.

Starting in 1972, the club has conducted a Sunday night barbeque at the Beach in summer, typically with about three hundred in attendance for dinner, and Sunday night dinner in the clubhouse during the winter, with a variety of themes to entice the children. In summer, dinner is served in the clubhouse on Wednesday, Thursday, and Saturday evenings, as well as Friday night at the Beach, in addition to the Sunday Beach cookout. During the winter, the two weekday evenings are conducted on a reciprocal basis with Piping Rock.

Duplicate bridge is another mutual endeavor undertaken with Piping Rock. Started in 1988 by The Creek's Jean Eakins and Cordy McCuaig and Piping Rock's Daphne Whitsell, the group, which consists of approximately sixteen women, meets twice a month from October through May, the first Sunday of the month at The Creek, the third Sunday at Piping Rock.

The clubhouse terrace

The Gibson Room

Our Staff

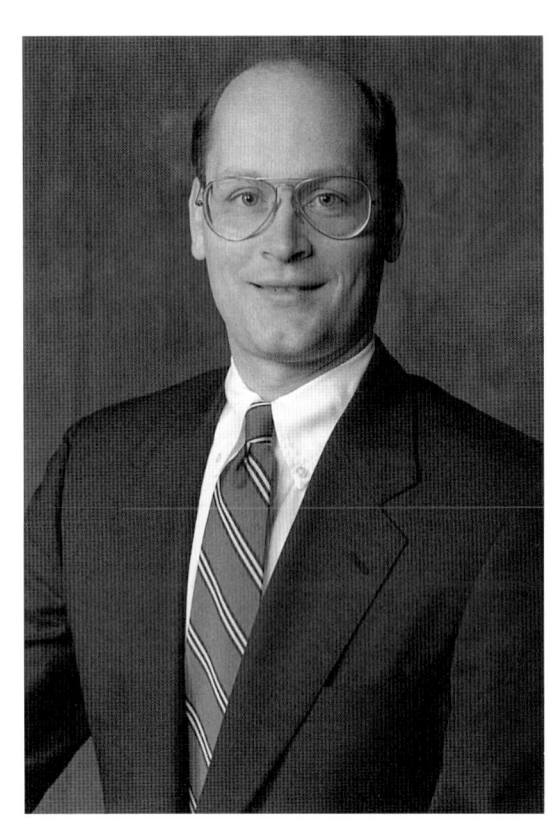

The Creek today offers its members a wide range of family activities. The atmosphere is friendly and informal, and this is enhanced by a marvelous staff known for its hospitality, a fact that is noted repeatedly by guests visiting from other clubs. The core of the staff is long standing, some life-long, and dedicated. The size of the staff ranges from 50 in the winter months to approximately 130 in season.

Heading the staff today, in title and by example, is Robert Stein, who has been with the club for twenty years. Robert started at The Creek in 1978 as a busboy at age fourteen, and then during his college years, served as a bartender and waiter at the Dormie House, Beach, and Main Clubhouse. In 1987 he was promoted to assistant manager and Beach manager and in 1993 was appointed general manager. Robert's dedication and hands-on operating style have contributed immeasurably to the smoothness and efficiency of all aspects of the club's operations.

Bill Jones, the club's golf course superintendent, started at The Creek in 1987. Just prior to coming to The Creek, Bill was the assistant superintendent at Merion Golf Club in Ardmore, Pennsylvania. Bill and his team played a key role in the successful restoration of the golf course in 1992.

Our assistant club manager and Beach manager is John Harvey who first started at The Creek twenty-eight years ago as a caddie and then became a bartender in the Dormie House. He eventually became Dormie House manager and in 1993 was promoted to his current position. John is an integral part of all club operations and his friendly personality is a true asset to the club.

Assisting Bill Lewis and John Harvey is Alan Perez who is the manager of the Dormie House. Alan successfully oversees all operations of the Dormie House during the busy summer season and also the popular casual winter Dormie dining.

All too often there are unsung, behind-the-scenes heroes who are invaluable to the successful operation of any organization. The Creek is no exception. It is blessed with the presence of an office staff which is second to none in importance. The club's executive secretary is Lee Chapklin whose administrative talents are outstanding. Lee maintains current and complete records on all membership information, publishes and distributes all Executive and Board Meeting Minutes and performs countless other tasks, large and small, willingly and always with a welcome cheeriness.

The Creek's finances would not be in as fine a condition were it not for the expertise and dedication of Lorraine Lein-Casey who is the club's controller. Working closely with the club's general manager and treasurer, Lorraine insures that

General Manager Robert Stein

LEFT: The Main Clubhouse staff

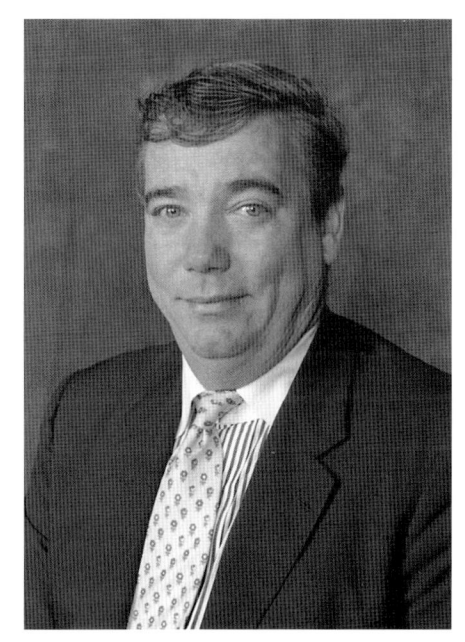

John Harvey, Assistant Manager

Golf Superintendent Bill Jones and friends

accuracy, timeliness, and efficiency are hallmarks of the club's financial status—qualities that are indispensable in the management of any organization with financial demands influenced by occasionally unpredictable business cycles. Lorraine and Lee are ably assisted by Rodney Johnsen and Marion Hahn.

The Creek's front desk staff also play an integral role in club operations. Marge Ruzicka is the club's primary receptionist. Marge successfully handles and coordinates all front desk operations and assists the administrative office staff with accounting functions. Marge is also responsible for the wonderful Christmas decorations at the club during the holidays. Assisting Marge at the front desk are George Mavrokefalos, Debbie Sorenson, and Connie Hay. A new era in club dining began this past year with the arrival of Executive Chef Craig Henne who brings wide experience in the culinary arts to his new assignment.

In celebrating the seventy-fifth anniversary of The Creek, we are proud to acknowledge those who have contributed so much over the years to the unique character and quality of life of The Creek.

The Creek 149

An Easter buffet

The office staff

> The club expresses its gratitude to those listed below on
> The Creek Honor Roll
> of at least ten years or more of service.
>
> | | |
> |---|---|
> | Bill Lewis | Clubhouse Manager 1947 |
> | Konrad Wolny | Greens 1950 |
> | Jeff Converse | Senior Lifeguard 1967 |
> | Angelo Stanco | Assistant Pool Director 1967 |
> | John Harvey | Assistant Manager 1970 |
> | Mary O'Hare | Waitress 1975 |
> | Ray D'Annolfo | Pool Director 1976 |
> | Marge Ruzicka | Receptionist 1976 |
> | Robert Stein | General Manager 1978 |
> | Lorraine Lein-Casey | Controller 1978 |
> | Lee Chapklin | Secretary 1980 |
> | Jesus Perez | Maintenance 1983 |
> | Nancy Cowley | Captain 1983 |
> | Connie Hay | Receptionist 1984 |
> | Alan Perez | Dormie House Manager 1986 |
> | Kathleen Harris | Waitress 1986 |
> | Bill Jones | Golf Superintendent 1987 |

The Creek 151

Epilogue

The publication of this history of The Creek does not signal the end of its remarkable story, but merely a pause along the way. For The Creek will live on in the spirit of future generations of member families whose love and respect for the club's traditions, as perpetuated by past members, will preserve the essence of the club as we know it today. It will differ only in the names of the members and their judicious adaptation to the future environment through change rooted in the club's traditions. Thus will the Creek always be—The Creek—a very special and unique place, both physically and spiritually.

It has been a distinct honor and pleasure for me to have worked on this history of the club. I thank Bill Kenny for asking me to do it; and I thank all those who so willingly assisted and contributed to the project. My special thanks to Bill Quirin whose dedication and tireless effort are reflected throughout the book. His contributions, and those of everyone involved were clearly a labor of love.

DONALD J. SHEA
October 1998

Appendices

Officers

William F. Kenny III
President

John C. Thomas, Jr.
Vice President and Secretary

Robert C. Gardner
Vice President

James B. Patterson
Treasurer

Michael F. Schwerin
Assistant Treasurer

Executive Committee

Earl Ellis
Robert C. Gardner

William F. Kenny III
James F. Keresey

Richard W. Meyer, Jr.
James B. Patterson

Donald J. Sutherland
John C. Thomas, Jr.

George M. Wheatley III

Board of Governors

Francis L. Corcoran (Honorary)
Mrs. William S. Eakins (Honorary)
Earl Ellis
John R. Gambling
Robert C. Gardner
Stuart H. Hartmeyer

George J. Holland, Jr.
J. Mitchell Hull
Susan B. Karches
William F. Kenny III
James F. Keresey
Thomas A. Lewis, Jr.
Richard W. Meyer (Honorary)

Richard W. Meyer, Jr.
Mrs. Thomas F. X. Mullarkey
Innis O'Rourke, Jr.
James B. Patterson
Richard F. Powers III
Michael F. Schwerin
Alfred J. Seaman (Honorary)

Donald J. Shea
Ralph K. Smith, Jr.
Donald J. Sutherland
John C. Thomas, Jr.
Stephen C. Tuck
Jeffrey F. Welles
George M. Wheatley III

F. Dana Winslow, Jr.

Past Presidents

Clarence H. Mackay
1923–1938

Harvey D. Gibson
1941–1950

H. P. Davison
1950–1955

Artemus L. Gates
1955–1960

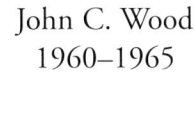

John C. Wood
1960–1965

William S. Renchard
1965–1970

George F. Baker, Jr.
1970–1975

Alfred J. Seaman
1975–1980

John O. Pickett, Jr.
1980–1983

John C. Jansing
1983–1987

Richard W. Meyer
1987–1991

James K. Keresey
1991–1995

William F. Kenny III
1995–present

154 The Creek

The Creek

A Pause along the Way
1923–1998

The Anniversary Book Committee

William F. Kenny III	Donald J. Shea	James F. Keresey
Honorary Chairman	Chairman	Innis J. O'Rourke, Jr.
		Co-Chairmen

Editorial Contributors

Mrs. Allan W. Ames	Mr. Howard J. Dirkes, Jr.	Mr. and Mrs. Harrison M. Knight	Mr. James B. Patterson
Mrs. William F. Bremer	Mrs. William S. Eakins	Mr. Alexander MacCormick	Mr. Robert Picoli
Mr. Lester E. Brion, Jr.	Mr. Stephen G. Fredericks	Mr. Malcolm McNair	Mr. Nicholas Salgo
Mr. Alec M. Choremi	Mr. Robert C. Gardner	Mr. Creighton McShane	Mr. Ralph K. Smith, Jr.
Mr. Peter Crisp	Mr. Prescott Jennings, Jr.	Mr. Richard W. Meyer	Mr. Donald J. Sutherland

Editorial Review Sub-Committee
Robert C. Gardner
William F. Kenny III
John C. Thomas, Jr.

Special Mention
Mr. Robert Stein
Mr. William Lewis
Mr. Jeffrey Converse
Mr. John Harvey

Professional Photographer
Larry C. Lambrecht
L. C. Photography
Westerly, Rhode Island

Golf Champions

Men

1945	I. O'Rourke	1972	J. F. Keresey
1946	K. H. Sheldon	1973	N. R. Ryan, Jr.
1947	K. H. Sheldon	1974	S. B. Gardiner
1948	A. K. Atkinson	1975	S. W. Titus
1949	A. M. Foster	1976	F. W. Hartmann
1950	B. C. Milner III	1977	N. R. Ryan, Jr.
1951	R. M. Balding	1978	S. W. Titus
1952	D. B. Tansill, Jr.	1979	S. W. Titus
1953	R. A. Graham, Jr.	1980	N. R. Ryan, Jr.
1954	D. B. Anthony	1981	J. J. Powers
1955	K. H. Sheldon	1982	S. W. Titus
1956	R. C. Townsend	1983	S. W. Titus
1957	A. F. Peck	1984	D. G. Barnes
1958	D. B. Anthony	1985	S. W. Titus
1959	J. F. Keresey	1986	S. W. Titus
1960	J. W. Waterbury	1987	S. W. Titus
1961	G. A, Nilson	1988	S. W. Titus
1962	R. C. Picoli	1989	L. F. Body V
1963	R. C. Townsend	1990	R. L. Doran
1964	J. F. Keresey	1991	J. J. Powers
1965	J. F. Keresey	1992	L. F. Body V
1966	D. S. Burr	1993	J. J. Powers
1967	D. S. Burr	1994	F. H. Edwards
1968	J. D. Robinson III	1995	D. G. Barnes
1969	J. O. Pickett, Jr.	1996	E. A. Scalamandre
1970	J. D. Robinson III	1997	J. J. Powers
1971	J. F. Keresey		

Women

1945	Mrs. V. D. Crisp	1972	Mrs. J. F. Keresey
1946	Mrs. Carl H. Sayre	1973	Mrs. C. C. Cullen
1947	Mrs. J. B. Balding	1974	Mrs. C. C. Cullen
1948	Mrs. J. B. Balding	1975	Mrs. C. C. Cullen
1949	Mrs. J. B. Balding	1976	Mrs. A. A. Ryan
1950	Mrs. J. B. Balding	1977	Mrs. C. C. Cullen
1951	Mrs. J. B. Balding	1978	Mrs. C. C. Cullen
1952	Mrs. J. B. Balding	1979	Mrs. C. C. Cullen
1953	Mrs. J. B. Balding	1980	Mrs. J. F. McCrary
1954	Mrs. T. R. Rudel	1981	Mrs. C. C. Cullen
1955	Mrs. J. B. Balding	1982	Mrs. J. M. Connors
1956	Mrs. J. B. Balding	1983	Mrs. J. M. Connors
1957	Mrs J. B. Balding	1984	Mrs. J. M. Connors
1958	Mrs. J. B. Balding	1985	Mrs. R. G. Broughton
1959	Mrs. J. B. Balding	1986	Mrs. J. M. Connors
1960	Mrs. E. H. Herzog	1987	Mrs. J. M. Connors
1961	Mrs. A. A. Ryan	1988	Mrs. J. M. Connors
1962	Mrs. A. A. Ryan	1989	Mrs. J. M. Connors
1963	Mrs. E. H. Herzog	1990	Mrs. T. M. Shogren
1964	Mrs. J. W. Harris	1991	Mrs. T. M. Shogren
1965	Mrs. E. H. Herzog	1992	Mrs. J. F. Keresey
1966	Mrs. J. F. Keresey	1993	Mrs. T. M. Shogren
1967	Mrs. F. E. Burke, Jr.	1994	Mrs. V. C. McCuaig
1968	Mrs. E. H. Herzog	1995	Mrs. D. A. Warner III
1969	Mrs. J. F. Keresey	1996	Mrs. D. A. Warner III
1970	Mrs. J. F. Keresey	1997	Mrs. S. G. Fredericks
1971	Mrs. J. F. Keresey		

Senior Golf Champions

Men

1991	D. P. Pearson	1995	L. F. Body IV
1992	D. P. Pearson	1996	E. Ellis
1993	P. Jennings, Jr.	1997	L. F. Body IV
1994	L. F. Body IV		

Women

1991	Mrs. W. F. Bremer	1995	Mrs. J. F. Keresey
1992	Mrs. F. S. Walker	1996	Mrs. F. S. Walker
1993	Mrs. M. J. Crimi	1997	Mrs. T. M. Shogren
1994	Mrs. J. F. Keresey		

Tennis Champions

Men's Singles Winners

1970	Wayne G. Quasha	1984	J. Christopher Muran
1971	A. George Dartt	1985	J. Christopher Muran
1972	Alan G. Quasha	1986	John S. Hutchins
1973	John S. Hutchins	1987	John S. Hutchins
1974	A. George Dartt	1988	John S. Hutchins
1975	Alexander A. Volz	1989	G. M. Wheatley, III
1976	Alexander A. Volz	1990	G. M. Wheatley, III
1977	John S. Hutchins	1991	Duncan W. Riefler
1978	Alexander A. Volz	1992	G. M. Wheatley, III
1979	Alexander M. Anderson	1993	G. M. Wheatley, III
1980	Paul L. Cranis	1994	Alan G. Quasha
1981	Alexander M. Anderson	1995	David F. Harrington
1982	Alexander A. Volz	1996	Marcus D. Hurlbut
1983	Alexander M. Anderson	1997	David F. Harrington

Women's Singles Winners

1970	Mrs. D. B. Riefler	1984	Mrs. A. M. C. MacCormick
1971	Mrs. S. S. Walker	1985	Mrs. M. Broughton
1972	Mrs. D. B. Riefler	1986	Mrs. M. Broughton
1973	Mrs. J. C. Jansing	1987	Mrs. G. H. Bullen
1974	Mrs. C. C. Cullen	1988	Mrs. S. H. Hartmeyer
1975	Mrs. C. C. Cullen	1989	Mrs. S. H. Hartmeyer
1976	Mrs. C. C. Cullen	1990	Mrs. S. H. Hartmeyer
1977	Mrs. C. C. Cullen	1991	Mrs. R. K. Mullarkey
1978	Miss Barbara A. Riefler	1992	Mrs. S. H. Hartmeyer
1979	Miss Linda H. Riefler	1993	Mrs. S. H. Hartmeyer
1980	Miss Linda H. Riefler	1994	Mrs. S. H. Hartmeyer
1981	Mrs. D. A. Warner	1995	Mrs. S. H. Hartmeyer
1982	Mrs. A. M. C. MacCormick	1996	Mrs. S. H. Hartmeyer
1983	Mrs. A. A. Volz	1997	Mrs. S. H. Hartmeyer

Paddle Tennis Champions

Men

1967	L. L. Marshall, Jr. T. B. Smith, Jr.	1976	A. Volz D. Warner
1968	J. F. Keresey L. L. Marshall, Jr.	1977	P. Cranis F. Williams
1969	A. G. Dartt C. A. Powers	1978	C. McShane T. B. Smith, Jr.
1970	J. F. Keresey C. J. Reid, Jr.	1979	D. A. Warner III A. A. Volz
1971	R. C. Gardner J. J. Devendorf	1980	G. M. Wheatley, Jr. G. M. Wheatley III
1972	R. C. Gardner J. J. Devendorf	1981	C. McShane A. A. Volz
1973	R. C. Gardner D. B. Riefler	1982	A. A. Volz D. A. Warner III
1974	T. B. Smith, Jr. C. McShane	1983	A. G. Dartt G. M. Wheatley III
1975	R. C. Gardner D. B. Riefler	1984	B. W. D. Betes B. J. H. K. Belt

Women

1967	Mrs. J. C. Jansing Mrs. D. B. Riefler	1976	Mrs. C. C. Cullen Mrs. J. F. Keresey
1968	Mrs. J. C. Jansing Mrs. J. B. Hartmeyer	1977	Mrs. D. B. Riefler Mrs. S. S. Walker
1969	Mrs. J. C. Jansing Mrs. R. C. Gardner	1978	Mrs. D. B. Riefler Mrs. S. S. Walker
1970	Mrs. J. C. Jansing Mrs. J. B. Hartmeyer	1979	Mrs. J. C. Jansing Mrs. S. S. Walker
1971	Mrs. R. K. Smith, Jr. Mrs. S. S. Walker	1980	Mrs. D. B. Riefler Mrs. C. C. Cullen
1972	Mrs. R. K. Smith, Jr. Mrs. S. S. Walker	1981	Mrs. C. C. Cullen Mrs. R. C. Gardner
1973	Mrs. R. K. Smith, Jr. Mrs. S. S. Walker	1982	Mrs. C. C. Cullen Mrs. R. C. Gardner
1974	Mrs. R. K. Smith, Jr. Mrs. S. S. Walker	1983	Mrs. G. H. Bullen Mrs. S. S. Walker
1975	Mrs. J. B. Hartmeyer Mrs. R. K. Smith, Jr.	1984	Mrs. J. B. Minnick Mrs. C. C. Powers, Jr.

Croquet Champions

Singles

1996 J. R. Bartholomew

1997 J. R. Bartholomew

Doubles

1996 H. H. Bartholomew
J. R. Bartholomew

1997 J. R. Bartholomew
W. D. Wylie

Squash Club Champions

Men

1987	J. S. Hutchins	1993	S. H. Hartmeyer
1988	J. S. Hutchins	1994	G. T. Frank
1989	J. F. Welles	1995	J. F. Welles
1990	J. F. Welles	1996	J. F. Welles
1991	J. F. Welles	1997	J. F. Welles
1992	J. F. Welles	1998	J. F. Welles

Women

1986	Miss Mimi T. French	1995	Mrs. S. H. Hartmeyer
1988	Miss Linda B. Riefler	1996	Mrs. S. H. Hartmeyer
1990	Mrs. D. Wagstaff III	1997	Miss Sarah Bartholomew
1993	Miss Caroline C. Jansing	1998	Mrs. S. H. Hartmeyer
1994	Mrs. S. H. Hartmeyer		

James F. Keresey Bowl
Squash Member-Guest Men

1988	J. F. Keresey / J. Havens	1994	G. T. Frank / W. D. Baumann
1989	J. E. Carney, Jr. / H. Grace	1995	J. F. Keresey / C. Caulkins
1990	J. F. Keresey / G. Burton	1996	G. M. Wheatley III / G. G. Dewey
1991	S. H. Hartmeyer / T. Megear	1997	R. W. Hagner / N. J. Pirozzi
1992	D. W. Riefler / F. S. vonStade III	1998	R. W. Hagner / N. J. Pirozzi
1993	D. W. Riefler / F. S. vonStade III		

Bowling Championship

Men

1947	E. T. Fox, Jr.	1973	J. Carney, Jr.
1948	B. C. Milner III	1974	J. Carney, Jr.
1949	B. C. Milner III	1975	J. Carney, Jr.
1950	B. C. Milner III	1976	J. Carney, Jr.
1951	B. C. Milner III		S. Feminella
1952	B. C. Milner III	1977	S. Feminella
1953	H. V. Richard	1978	D. C. Trautman
1954	H. V. Richard	1979	S. Feminella
1955	H. V. Richard	1980	S. Feminella
1956	Bruce Brodie	1981	S. Feminella
1957	B. C. Milner III	1982	N. R. Ryan, Jr.
1958	B. C. Milner III	1983	N. R. Ryan, Jr.
1959	Raymond French	1984	D. C. Trautman
1960	C. J. Werber	1985	S. S. Meyer
1961	C. J. Werber	1986	R. Meyer, Jr.
1962	C. J. Werber	1987	S. Feminella
1963	H. V. Richard	1988	R. Meyer, Jr.
1964	B. C. Milner III	1989	D. Meyer
1965	R. French	1990	E. Ellis
1966	J. Carney, Jr.	1991	E. Ellis
1967	B. C. Milner III	1992	D. Meyer
1968	J. Carney, Jr.	1993	R. Meyer, Jr.
1969	J. McMillen, Jr.	1994	E. Ellis
1970	H. V. Richard	1995	D. Meyer
1971	H. V. Richard	1996	R. Meyer, Jr.
1972	H. V. Richard	1997	R. Meyer, Jr.

Women

1947	Mrs. B. C. Milner III	1972	Mrs. Robert G. McKeon, Jr.
1948	Mrs. C. M. Deland, Jr.	1973	Mrs. H. A. Brown
1949	Mrs. C. M. Deland, Jr.	1974	Mrs. H. A. Brown
1950	Mrs B. Brodie	1975	Mrs. G. C. Meyer
1951	Mrs B. Brodie	1976	Mrs. G. C. Meyer
1952	Mrs. H. V. Richard	1977	Mrs. G. C. Meyer
1953	Mrs B. Brodie	1978	Mrs. G. C. Meyer
1954	Mrs. H. V. Richard	1979	Mrs. G. C. Meyer
1955	Mrs. B. C. Milner III	1980	Mrs. J. W. Gillies
1956	Mrs. J. Austin	1981	Mrs. J. W. Gillies
1957	Mrs. B. C. Milner III	1982	Mrs. G. C. Meyer
1958	Mrs. B. C. Milner III	1983	Mrs. G. C. Meyer
1959	Mrs B. Brodie	1984	No Winner
1960	Mrs. B. C. Milner III	1985	Mrs. G. C. Meyer
1961	Mrs. H. S. Nelson	1986	Mrs. G. C. Meyer
1962	Mrs. B. Brodie	1987	Mrs. R. W. Meyer, Jr.
1963	Mrs. G. C. Meyer	1988	Mrs. G. C. Meyer
1964	Mrs. J. V. Meyer	1989	Mrs. S. J. Patterson, Jr.
1965	Mrs. B. C. Milner III	1990	Mrs. G. C. Meyer
1966	Mrs. G. C. Meyer	1991	Mrs. S. J. Patterson, Jr.
1967	Mrs. J. V. Meyer		
1968	Mrs. G. C. Meyer		
	Mrs. S. Patterson		
1969	Mrs. G. C. Meyer		
1970	Mrs. G. C. Meyer		
1971	Mrs. G. C. Meyer		